PERMISSION

to

DREAM

From a Refugee Camp to Owning a
Multimillion-Dollar Real Estate Empire

WENDY HANG

ISBN: 978-1-958667-00-2 (Paperback)
ISBN: 978-1-958667-01-9 (Hardcover)

DEDICATION

To everyone who has ever made an impact on my life
– you know who you are.

THANK YOU!

CONTENT WARNING

THIS BOOK CONTAINS content that might be troubling to some readers, including, but not limited to, language some might find offensive and domestic violence. Please be mindful of these possible triggers and seek assistance if needed.

Table of Contents

INTRODUCTION

"If you are not willing to learn,
no one can help you.
If you are determined to learn,
no one can stop you."

— Zig Ziglar

We all have a story, a truth about our lives that is unique. I grew up in a refugee camp in Ban Vinai, Thailand. My family was one of several thousand refugees who had fled Laos, wading through the Mekong River into Thailand for safety. From there, we moved to another refugee camp before coming to America in 1988. At seven years old, I faced a whole new world, one where I didn't speak the language or know the customs but where I believed all of my dreams could come true. As a little Hmong girl, I had no idea what it meant to have to fight for all those dreams swirling around in my head.

But I am a fighter by nature, and I learned, on my first day of school, to pursue my dreams with determination until I achieved my goals. On my journey I met dream killers and vision thieves, disguised as teachers, elders, a husband – and life! I failed miserably and often but I kept moving forward. There were barriers set up by society which said I was a lesser mortal because I am a woman and a minority. Equally, there were the walls I built around myself to protect me from the wounds of racism, domestic violence, and gender inequality, both in my Hmong community and in the world around me. The walls I built to block things out also kept me blocked in, incapable of living my best life.

But fight I must. I had to learn to overcome the struggles within myself and in my environment. I had to learn to elevate my mindset by surrounding myself with people who thought and achieved at a higher level. I got lost along the way, blinded by the mirage of seeking money and possessions as a cure for all pain. I fell from the highest heights to the lowest lows, climbed back up, and got dragged down again. But I never gave up. I shifted my focus to changing me instead of blaming others, and as I self-evaluated, I overcame my core issue — the self-doubt that was holding me hostage.

Much of my ethos came from my family who believed in the value of hard work and education, not dreams. I didn't come from wealth. There was no investment capital sitting in a bank somewhere, no inheritance when I came of age. I was definitely not born with a silver spoon in my mouth. It was with my hands and my heart that I built an empire, literally starting from the ground up. It wasn't easy. As someone who comes from very humble beginnings, it was the greatest challenge of my life.

How did it all happen? Let me unravel my story. My aim is to encourage and inspire you to reach for the stars. You may be facing that same challenge because you may be in a position where you feel like you can't get up, you can't make it. You may have a similar story to mine. Yours, too, will be unique. One thing remains the same — you can get up. No matter where you are, no matter what the circumstances, you can develop the steely resolve to challenge and disrupt the world around you.

But it must start with a vision and a passion. I want to demonstrate to you by virtue of my own life and the obstacles I faced how to hold onto the vision you have for your life until you see it come true. My goal is to help you believe that you can do anything you put your mind to. You don't have to be afraid of failure. Embrace it because it's your best teacher. Know that it's okay to fail or fall as long as you get back up and into the game again. The world won't end when you make a mistake. It doesn't matter what your background is, where you come from, or even how you got where you are today.

With this book, you will discover the foundation for building the life you dream about. I hope you will be inspired, energized, and activated to do the things you need to do to move your life in the direction of your goals. You will learn to see yourself in the light of who you want to be. You will learn the value of goal setting and getting the right mindset. You will see the importance of passion, perseverance, and hard work. You will learn to apply financial principles of investing rather than consuming and living paycheck to paycheck.

We all have the same power inherent in us to achieve our goals, including wealth, as long as we allow ourselves that liberty. Life is a gift, and it is up to us what we make of it. Make your life a great story, a grand journey, a life of love, joy, health, wealth, and fulfillment. Give yourself permission to dream.

CHAPTER ONE

HUMBLE BEGINNINGS

How did the Hmong people end up as refugees in America? For centuries, the Hmong people have been a people without a country. The Hmong lived in China in 2700 B.C. Conflicts arose with the Han Dynasty in the 19th century that caused some Hmong people to migrate into the mountains of Vietnam, Laos, and Thailand. There they tried to maintain their cultural identity and their belief in freedom, but because of the constant wars and genocide perpetuated against the Hmong by various factions, the Hmong were never able to establish their own government. They had lived in Southwestern China for thousands of years until the mid-1600s, when the Chinese began limiting the freedom they so prized.

The Hmong people were essentially farmers who lived off the land. During the Vietnam war, also known as the Second Indochina War, the CIA visited the Hmong and found them a great asset to the United States military because they knew the terrain. They were familiar with areas that the US needed to protect and defend. So the CIA enlisted the Hmong people, befriended them, and trained the men* in guerilla warfare and military rescue missions. In fact, several of the Hmong fought side by side with the US military on the battlefield. They blocked the Ho Chi Minh trail to enable American crossings. They defended radar stations. They gave their lives believing America would win in the war against communism and they would be able to maintain their freedom. But ultimately the Americans didn't win the war, and the Hmong people, some still on the battlefield, were left to fend for themselves when the US military forces pulled out.

When the communist leaders learned that the Hmong had worked with the US Central Intelligence Agency (CIA), and had also fought for the US, they began a campaign of genocide, scouring the mountains for any remaining Hmong people. The Vietnamese communists burned down their small villages, killing men, women, and children. As the Hmong tried to flee their homeland to other countries, there were shots fired from the air, killing them. They bombed and gassed many who were left hiding in the mountains. They had become a hunted people.

This is not a story recorded in the history books. It is one very few tell except the elders who remember. They remember the building of the Great Wall of China meant to block out Hmong rebellion. They remember crossing the Yellow River. Those who did not submit to the communist party were killed and others forced into labor camps after North Korea won the war in May of 1975. The Hmong peoples were refugees in Thailand for over 20 years before being allowed into America as political refugees. On May 23, 1975, the 94th United States Congress enacted the Indochina Migration Refugee Assistance Act with the goal of relocating Hmong and Laotian immigrants after the Vietnam War. As a result, thousands of Hmong people now live across the United States, with the majority in California, Minnesota, and Wisconsin. There are also Hmong people in Canada, Europe and Australia.

The Crossing

My parents came from a small village in the Pak Ngum/Naxay area of Laos. They were both young and had never met prior to their arranged marriage in 1973. Neither of them knew what they wanted or what the future held.

After they were married, they moved to a village in the Sam Neua area. They lived there for some time before moving on. Because of social and political unrest in the country largely due to the Viet Cong, they had to keep moving, trying to find a safe place to raise a family.

In South Vietnam, Laos, and Cambodia, there was an armed communist revolutionary group known as the Viet Cong. During the Vietnam War, it fought alongside North Vietnam against the governments of South Vietnam and the United States.

Early one morning in 1979, news spread through their small Laotian village that the Viet Cong were coming. My parents feared for theirs and their children's lives. They immediately decided along with several other villagers that they would go to Thailand where they could be safe. Neighbors cried and whispered among each other, "There isn't anywhere else for us to run to."

What stood between my family and safety was the Mekong River. May to November is the monsoon season in the Mekong Delta, and monsoon winds can sweep across the land at 70 miles per hour or more. Monsoon rains account for about 99% of the area's yearly rainfall. While these rains are good for the rice industry, they are life-threatening when one has to cross the river to safety.

With great haste my parents, along with several other families, gathered the bare necessities, strapped the children on their backs, and ran to hide in the jungle, leaving everything else they owned behind. All day and into the night they trudged, sober and quiet, through the jungle towards the Mekong River.

The Mekong River is the sixth largest river in Asia measuring about one mile wide, and the twelfth largest river in the world. When its rivers overflow from May to November, crashing monsoon winds can easily take whole families under. My parents hid in the dense forest till nightfall. A squall was brewing. Driving rain and thunder pounded the earth. Winds of up to 60 and 70 miles per hour shook the trees. The people of the village had been told not to idle too long by the shores. They knew they wouldn't survive another day if they stayed put, so they cut bamboo stems to make floating rafts, two bamboo bundles per person. They used ropes, straps, and whatever they could find to tie around their waist and to each other. Not many people knew how to swim. The ropes were tied to ensure that family members weren't left behind or drowned. If they could get to the opposite shore, they would have a chance. Despite the torrential rains, the high winds, and the darkness that surrounded them, they all waded into the river.

Minutes after they entered the water, the enormous currents generated by the strong winds forced everyone backwards. Again, they strained forward but their bodies were no match for the swirling angry currents that rose around them.

Defeated, tired, and afraid, they went back to the riverbank to wait out the storm. When the storm died down, they reentered the river pressing forward again. Strung together, they swam all night long. Despite being pushed back time and time again by the wind and waves, they kept moving mile by tedious, treacherous mile, until they crossed over to Thailand the next morning.

Not everyone made it to shore that morning. Several drowned trying to cross the river. Countless men, women, and children died that night and the many nights before and after.

Life in a Refugee Camp

My family's life had not been an easy one. That fateful night of the Mekong crossing, their only hope was to get across the river to Thailand's refugee camp before the Viet Cong could track them down. Fortune had not been kind to the 100,000 others who were captured and killed trying to flee Laos. Over 50,000 more men, women, and children died in their attempt to cross the Mekong River (Hmong Association of Washington, 2010).

My family and the rest who survived the crossing walked until they came to a path that led into a small Thai village. There they were greeted by a group of people who recognized them as Hmong escaping genocide in Laos. Some of the Thais were kind and generous, offering the Hmong survivors food and water. Other Thai villagers, however, robbed the fleeing Hmong of everything they had of value. They took every cent of the little bit of money my parents had.

Hours later, Thai soldiers arrived in large military transport vehicles to take the Hmong people to a holding station. There they were processed, given paperwork, and housed. About a month later, with their paperwork approved, they were transported to the Ban Vinai Refugee Camp.

Ban Vinai was originally built in 1975 as a holding center for the 12,000 refugees who lived in the highlands that were fleeing communist rule in Laos. The population in the camp grew quickly to 45,000 from the period of 1975 to 1992, most of whom were Hmong people. What was once a refugee camp became a village for thousands of families from Laos, Vietnam, and Cambodia.

I was born in Ban Vinai a few years after my parents arrived there. They had other children before me who hadn't survived the escape to Thailand. The constant moving and running from one village to the next coupled with the extremely harsh conditions had taken its toll on their offspring.

Ban Vinai was my first home. We lived in a massive, corrugated iron building with six other families. Our dwelling had dirt floors, a living and cooking space that all the families shared, and a bedroom for each family. There was no furniture except for the few small chairs that the men crafted out of wood. Most of the families in our home were aunts, uncles, and distant cousins. Some houses in the camp were built by the refugees themselves, with lightly thatched and metal roofs. The concrete buildings were used for healthcare centers, administration buildings, and dormitories.

Dirt was the one thing that pervaded the camp — dirt floors, dirt roads, and mounds of dirt everywhere. When it rained it could get pretty muddy. As children, we used our imagination to draw pictures in the dirt with sticks we found on the ground. We used stones and rocks to create a game similar to the American game of jacks. We arranged the sticks on the ground, then we would throw a rock up in the air and try to gather as many sticks as possible before it fell, catching the rock in the same hand as the sticks. We created all kinds of games and makeshift competitions. Like other children we would run through the camp playing, laughing, and chasing one another.

A refugee camp is a holding place for those whose lives are threatened by war, political upheaval, and distress. It is not built for convenience. Surrounding Ban Vinai were walls, barbed wire fences, and Thai soldiers. Leaving the camp for your own recognizance was out of the question. Food was rationed. Sometimes the rations were moldy and stale. Clothes were donated by several organizations. There was no electricity, indoor toilets, or running water. There was no sewage system, so it was not uncommon to see excrement and urine on the ground as we played. Sickness and death were a part of everyday life.

I never knew life outside the walls of the camp until I was about five years old and my parents took me to a nearby theater. It was a wonderful treat. I don't remember what the name of the movie was or the characters who played in it but it was the first American movie I had ever seen, and it made a huge impact on me. That movie was the catalyst that inspired me to dream bigger than I ever had before. In it I saw a family in a big, beautiful house. The children were riding bikes to school. The parents had their own car. Life for them was exciting and wonderful. As we watched the movie screen, my parents told me that we would be going to that place someday.

I was genuinely intrigued by what my parents had told me and I couldn't stop thinking about the creature comforts of the family in the movies. Could life really be like that for us one day? I believed it. My parents said we would go there, and I believed we could. When my parents got busy with my newborn baby brother, I would ask my grandmother for one baht, the cost of a theater ticket to go to the movies. While most children would have used that money for candy, I ran to the movies. I would sit and watch that same movie over and over again, dreaming of the day my family would go to America.

My parents had one thing many people lose when they go through hardship. They had an enormous amount of hope. They hoped they could live in peace in the land of their fathers. Living in the Ban Vinai Camp, they hoped for a better life for their children. No matter how long it took, they would continue to keep that hope alive in themselves, and in their children.

Determined to Learn

You can imagine how difficult it was living in a refugee camp especially for the adults. Many people were there so long, they lost hope of ever leaving. They felt like prisoners, trapped in an atmosphere of discouragement, loss of loved ones, and poverty. But I was a dreamer. The movie I saw had fueled a deep and growing desire in me to have and become more even when others struggled to believe it was possible. My parents said it could happen and I believed them. But life in a refugee camp is not about dreaming. It is about hard work and surviving through the overcrowding and lack. How do you support a dream in that? The answer is you never give up.

At the Ban Vinai camp, I was an inquisitive child who loved to learn. I was too young to go to school but I would walk to school with my older cousins pretending to be a student. When they would go into the school building, I would often stand by the window and try to follow along with their lessons.

In February 1988, my family finally made it on the list to go to America. It had been nine years since that fateful river crossing. I was excited. We were in the process of taking the next step which meant moving to the Phanat Nikhom Transition Camp in the Chonburi Province of Thailand. Phanat Nikhom was the largest refugee camp in the world. It too was surrounded by barbed wire fences, the same concrete walls, and a continual slew of soldiers guarding the area.

We packed up what things we could carry with us, said goodbye to our friends and family left behind, and boarded the large, crowded buses with other families who had been lucky enough to make the list.

The purpose of the transition camp was to prepare families who were going to America to assimilate the new culture. The camp itself wasn't very different from our home in Ban Vinai with a few exceptions. There were rows and rows of cement buildings. There were medical huts, buildings for school, and funeral huts. The adults were required to learn to read and write in English and Hmong. They were also trained for various jobs, primarily those in which they would be paid lower wages.

My older cousins attended a nearby school but I was still too young to attend. I was determined to learn to speak and write in English. So instead of staying at home, I went to observe my parents in their classes from an outside window. I watched my mom and dad repeat the words the instructor said. Standing outside at the window, I repeated after them and followed along with the lessons. My mother saw me standing outside the window and shooed me away, mouthing for me to go home. I just ignored her and stayed.

From March to July of 1988, I would go stand outside the adult's classroom almost every single day. I followed along with any lessons that captured my interest. I eventually picked up a few words, learned how to count to ten, and could recite my ABC. One day I picked up one of my mother's Hmong and English books and started reading. I didn't know all of the words but could decipher most of it.

I was finally allowed to attend school with my cousins and the other children when I was seven years old. You can't imagine how overjoyed I was at the prospect of really being a part of a class. Like a kid in a candy store, I remember lining up outside before class giddy with excitement. The teachers went to all the students to check their fingernails every morning. I had to hold out both my hands, palms facing up, nails curled upwards so the teacher could easily inspect them for dirt. If your nails were dirty, the teacher would smack your hands hard with a stick. My first lesson was to keep my nails clean, at least before I went to school. I didn't care what I had to do or what it took for me to remain a part of the class. I was delighted to finally have my own little desk.

Two months later it was my family's turn to go to America. We had lived in Phanat Nikhom for seven months. As I said goodbye to my friends and goodbye to the school, I didn't feel any sadness. I was getting closer to my dream and I knew more adventures were about to roll out for me in America.

In October 1992, the Ban Vinai camp shut down. The remaining inhabitants who were qualified to go to some place in Europe, Canada, or the United State were transported to transition camps. Those who didn't qualify were sent back to Laos or other camps.

CHAPTER TWO

A FOREIGN LAND

"While every refugee's story is different and their anguish personal, they all share a common thread of uncommon courage — the courage not only to survive but to persevere and rebuild their shattered lives."

Antonio Guterres

The Indochina Migration Refugee Assistance Act passed by President Gerald Ford had helped over 200,000 refugees to relocate in the United States. Agencies like the United States Catholic Conference, the

International Rescue Committee, the American Council for Nationalities Service, and several others helped to place and finance the scores of new people arriving at America's shores.

Going to America

My parents, my two younger brothers, my dad's sister, my grandmother, and I arrived in the United States in September of 1988. I was seven, and my younger brothers were one and two years old. None of us had ever been on an airplane before. The airport itself was an adventure. We boarded an international flight full of other Hmong people going to the United States for the first time. My mom and dad held my little brothers on their laps. I wanted the window seat so I could look outside. Unlike my parents and other adults on the plane, I was a child who didn't have any fear. I wanted to see everything, to experience it all. I was going to make sure I didn't miss anything.

My grandmother, aunt, and my mom were very nauseous as were many other Hmong people on the plane. Maybe the queasiness was due to nerves or fear. They were leaving behind everything they had known. Hmong people drew spiritual strength from their ancestral lands and now they were leaving all of that for a strange place with strange customs. None of us was fluent in English. The only phrase we knew how to say with any confidence was, "Hello, my name is …" Psychologically, it was a great deal to take in.

My little face was glued to the cabin's plexiglass window the entire flight. Being in a plane, high above the ground, floating among the clouds in the sky fascinated me. I could see the mountains and cities below, the lights mesmerizing on a gorgeous backdrop in the night sky.

The total flight time from Bangkok International Airport to the airport in Seattle, Washington, was about 16 hours. We were on a connecting flight and Seattle, Washington was our first stop. The downtown Seattle skyline was stunning, the buildings seeming to grow in front of my eyes as we prepared to land. Cars lined up in row upon row coming and going back and forth on the freeway. So many, just like I had seen in the movies. In the air and on the ground the multitude of buildings looked tall and graceful against the sky. I had never seen anything like it. It all felt like a dream. I was speechless as we prepared to deplane.

We said goodbye to some of our friends and family from Phanat Nikhom. Our families hugged and cried as we parted. We were going to California and had to catch another flight to Sacramento. Other friends and family were headed to Minnesota. We didn't have much money and travel was expensive. We didn't know if we would ever see each other again.

When we landed in Sacramento, my mom's brother, Uncle Houa, met us at the airport. It had been several years since my mother had last seen her brother. There weren't a lot of words that passed between them, but tears were plentiful. It was a relief to be hugged by someone familiar in a place where so much was unknown. There were plenty more hugs to go around that day.

Life in a refugee camp had been disheartening. Now the challenge of assimilation in a country and culture that weren't very accepting of Asian immigrants could sometimes be just as discouraging. Many Americans were politically opposed to the financial assistance refugees received. Some protested that it was unfair to Americans needing aid as the country was facing an economic downturn after the Vietnam war. The American loss of over 58,000 young men in that war agitated those who saw Asian immigrants as enemies. They did not know, of course, about the 30,000 Hmong soldiers who had served and died on behalf of the United States. This had not been a part of American history. As a result, many of the Hmong, Cambodian, and Vietnamese men, women, and children were met with hostility and racism.

My parents rented an apartment in West Sacramento, California, where a lot of other Hmong families lived. We didn't have a lot when we came to this country, but we had each other: family and community. In Hmong culture, that is everything.

My parents worked hard, and they were very frugal with what they earned. They bought clothes, household items, and other necessities from the Goodwill store. There was a church down the street where they would go to pick up donated clothing and food. The younger children wore hand me downs. I had one pair of shoes that I wore every day. I didn't know what Nike, Adidas, or any other branded items were. I was just satisfied that my parents made sure we had what we needed. Our clothes weren't ripped or torn, and we had enough to eat. On special occasions we enjoyed a treat of candy or chips. In my mind, I was already living out the dream.

I quickly made friends in our neighborhood and was overjoyed that I would soon be starting in an American school. I was genuinely thrilled and excited on that first day. But from day one I learned that looking and sounding different was cause for mistreatment from cruel young children.

I was in the first grade. A group of girls spoke to me. I didn't understand what they were saying and didn't know how to respond. They looked from one to the other and laughed out loud. They moved on but I felt that their constant chatter was about me. I wished I understood. If I did, I could stand up for myself. I had never been afraid of doing that. But I was confused. They didn't send us to school with interpreters, so we had to find our own way. From that point on, I was determined to be fluent in English and I focused my attention on my studies. I picked things up quickly in school, so quickly that three months into first grade, I was moved to the second grade. By the end of the second grade, I was fluent in English.

Despite their harrowing journey, the Hmong people who could not speak the language and were not readily accepted, saw America as a land of great opportunity. Their old life was gone. The new one was vastly different from what they were accustomed to. Many Hmong children were bullied and mistreated in school. We looked different, sounded different, and arrived on the heels of a critical moment in US history. But these brave Hmong people dared to dream of a better life in a new world, even when dreaming was not a part of their tradition. All they knew was that when you come from nothing, you have nothing more to lose.

Growing and Gardening

Most marriages were arranged in Hmong tradition. Though my parents knew nothing about each other when they were first married, they committed to making their marriage work. They were young, strong, and fiercely determined. In our culture there is no such thing as divorce. Nothing is more important than the relationship you have with your family. The larger the family, the better the support system.

Families not only lived together, but they also worked together and move as one unit bonded by interdependence. They helped to keep one another safe, took care of the elders in their household and in the community, and upheld a commitment to their specific clan. Being of an independent spirit, this was sometimes a problem for me.

My dad was tall with a dark tan complexion, thick black hair, and deep brown eyes. He was an extremely conscientious and industrious man who always kept busy finding ways to make a better life for his family. He wasn't home much during the week because he chose to work a lot of overtime. When he wasn't working, he was helping one relative or another. He never hesitated to help anyone who asked and was respected by everyone.

There weren't many good paying jobs available to immigrants, especially if you couldn't speak much English. Companies would hire those who were undocumented and pay them low wages, sometimes treating them badly and threatening deportation. Even those who had papers were still hired at low wages for jobs that most people didn't want. My father got paid $6.00 an hour to work at a computer manufacturing plant. In 1988 the minimum wage in the United States was $3.35 per hour, so $6.00 was pretty good.

But that was not enough for my father. He wanted more for his family, so he worked tirelessly. It seemed as though he never rested. Monday through Friday he would leave the house in his dress pants and dress shirt before five in the evening and not return most times until 1:00 or 2:00 in the early morning. He would get a little sleep then get up early to take us children to school.

The most important priority for their children as far as my parents were concerned was getting a good education. They hoped we would one day go to college and make something of ourselves. This was true of many Hmong families. It was the one chance of economic and social advancement in America. My father never said we had to be doctors or lawyers, but school was top priority, and he was strict about our attendance, so much so that I had perfect attendance all the way up to sixth grade.

No matter how busy my dad was, he would make sure he personally dropped us off at school and picked us up every day. I envied the other children who got to walk home from school. I wanted to walk home with my new friends too. I would often hide from my father and then walk home with my childhood buddies. My parents would be worried sick. By the time I got home my father would be furious. As a child, how could I understand that his anger was based on fear? The United States was a big place and if someone carried me off he wouldn't have known where to begin to look.

It was not for nothing that my parents feared their children would be kidnapped or abducted. I didn't know anything about bride kidnapping in Hmong culture. Even though such an act would have been considered a crime in America, my parents may not have understood that, nor would they have wanted to call the police for an infraction that was native to their culture.

My mother is petite with a round face, fair skin, and long black hair that she usually wears in a neat bun at the nape of her neck. She's one of the most resilient, resourceful, and determined women I know. Always soft-spoken but fierce at the same time, she is someone we children knew we could always go to whenever something disturbed us. As a traditional Hmong wife and homemaker, she cooked, cleaned, and took care of everything concerning the household. We never lacked in any area because of her devotion to her children. The death of a child is perhaps the single most devastating thing that can happen to a parent. A darkness, an emptiness enters your life that cannot be comforted. To this day, my mother never talks about the children she lost in Laos during the war — the memory is just too painful.

In Hmong families, women are traditionally homemakers and mothers. Little girls learn early how to cook, clean, and take care of children. Our socialization went beyond playing with dolls like American girls. It was full out conditioning for future responsibilities. Females were groomed for traditional roles and only those. I hated cooking and cleaning and my mother always teased me about my lack of skills in the kitchen. But, for me, I decided early that I wasn't going to be a servant to anyone.

"You're not a boy. If you don't learn to cook, how will you feed your husband one day when you get married?" she would ask.

"He can feed himself. Why do I need to feed him?" I responded. "Men have hands too."

"How will you feed your children?"

"Don't worry! Why do you worry so much? I'm not going anywhere. I'm going to live with you forever," I said jokingly.

"I won't be around forever. I'm worried one day you won't know how to feed your husband and your children."

"Then I guess we'll eat grass," I chuckled.

My mother sigh in disappointment and shook her head, "My dear child, what am I going to do with you?"

She said no one would ever marry me. If they did, they would send me back in three days because I couldn't cook. That didn't matter to me. I rebelled against the time-honored tradition of a woman's place.

I've always been a dreamer. I would lie in my bed staring at the ceiling, my head filled with a million ideas of things I could do, places I would one day visit, adventures I would have.

"Mao, come make rice," my mom would call from the kitchen. Everyone in my family calls me Mao. In Hmong it means tiny.

"Okay!" I responded without rising from my bed.

The dream was so much better than the reality, so I decided to stay there. Besides, I told myself, my mother had my grandmother and my aunt to help her cook. She didn't need me. By the time I dragged myself to the kitchen about two hours later, my grandmother had already made the rice. Of course, everyone scolded me but that didn't bother me in the least. Bored, I would shrug my shoulders and head back to my bedroom until it was time to set the dinner table.

My parents weren't the mushy type who said "I love you" at every turn. Nor were there a lot of hugs and kisses. Personal displays of affection were not the Hmong way. But we knew we were loved. Hmong show love by taking care of their children's needs and occasionally presenting them with gifts. Traditional Hmong men and women have specific roles with women as nurturers and caregivers and men as providers, responsible for decision making and finances. Respect for elders was expected.

Elders are highly regarded in our community because they carry the history of family and clan. Children are expected to take care of their aging parents just as their parents took care of them.

In Hmong families, everyone has a job to do. While our main job as children in the household was to get an education, there were still things to do around the house. On a typical day, my mom, grandma, and aunt were usually occupied with cooking, cleaning and caring for the younger children. There were seven of us altogether.

When my siblings and I were not in school, we would spend most of our time sitting in the living room watching cartoons. My dad thoroughly disliked those cartoons. He said watching them would make our brains turn to mush. Since I was the eldest, my task was to keep an eye on my siblings. I was an extremely active child and a little bit of a tomboy. I played hopscotch and Chinese jump rope with the girls but was a little more adventurous when playing with the boys. I enjoyed climbing trees, riding bikes, skateboarding, and jumping fences to explore the field beyond where we caught grasshoppers and dragonflies. I loved the outdoors. There were times when I ducked out on my babysitting duties and ran off to play outside with my friends. I would usually get a scolding afterward but that didn't bother in the least.

On the weekends, my dad and I would do the laundry at the local laundromat in a nearby strip mall. I loved going to the laundromat with him mostly because there was a vending machine there that had chips and candies. Dad always gave me fifty cents for helping and I would choose a snack from the machine. Doing laundry didn't seem like a chore because there was so much else to do while we were there. Sometimes while we were waiting for the clothes to dry, we would take a walk around the strip mall and window shop. Sometimes my younger brothers would accompany me and my father. We kept ourselves occupied racing to fold clothes fresh out of the dryer. The person who folded all the clothes in their pile first was the winner.

At the same time, I loved reading. One of my favorite places to visit on the weekend with my father and siblings was the library. We spent hours there listening to audio books and reading. I read *Charlotte's Web,* series books like *The Baby-Sitters Club* and *Sweet Valley High*, and *Little House on the Prairie*. My favorites, though, were books that contained anything and everything about ghosts, dragons, princesses, and the paranormal. I read teen horror fiction novels including R.L. Stine's *Goosebumps* series and the *Fear Street Saga*. As a child with a huge imagination, each book was an escape to an adventurous unknown world. In that world I could become whoever I wanted to be. I could be the princess or the dragon, the hero or the villain, and no one would judge me. I ran away in my mind to another place that made my heart race.

Though my father was stern when it came to our education, he was also a lot of fun. He loved to tell jokes and enjoyed a good laugh. More than that, he loved spending those rare moments with his children. We all knew we meant the world to him.

What was most consistent about our family chores was attending to the family garden. Hmong people were traditionally farmers, working the land for a living. My father started our family garden on a small plot of land close to our home. We grew green beans, cucumbers, red chili peppers, and several other vegetables that we used for ourselves and shared with other families in need, especially the elderly. There was always more than enough to share.

During the day while most of their children were in school, my parents tended the garden. In the morning after my father dropped us off, he and my mother would plant, weed, water, and pick vegetables for dinner.

Gardening was another one of those things I wasn't very fond of. Because we were older, my brothers and I helped out in the garden after school or on weekends. We watered, weeded, picked vegetables and bagged them for storage. It was always too hot, and I had long since lost my fascination with playing in the dirt. You couldn't get me to dig a hole or pull up weeds. I was terrified of worms and caterpillars, and everybody knew it. As much as I liked reading about horror and the paranormal, nothing scared me more than squirming earthworms and those fuzzy little creatures with a zillion legs who liked chewing on leaves. I refused to go anywhere near anything that looked like it might be a perfect haven for caterpillars.

The weather in Sacramento is perfect for year round farming so there was never a break in between for us. As soon as we harvested everything, it was time to till the ground again and plant new things. You can learn a great deal from gardening. It's a lot like life. Things are always growing or dying. There are weeds that have to be pulled up and ripped out, so they don't kill the potential of the good things that you're growing. There are always lessons to be learned from planting. What you allow to be planted in the fertile ground of your mind and heart can either reap a blessing of benefits or a horribly poor crop of regret.

Gardening is hard work, challenging even in the best of times. I watched my parents struggle to take care of us and vowed that I would work hard to support them so they would never again have to labor like they did. I wanted to do more, always more. I was determined to make a better life for me and for them. It would be many years before I learned the value in growing a garden with my family.

CHAPTER THREE

THE POWER OF POSSIBILITY

In the summer of 1992, my family and I moved to a different apartment complex, which meant a new school, new friends, and a new environment. Across the street, the rows of gleaming houses with their beautiful red tile roofs, enormous picture windows, fresh cut grass, and expertly landscaped yards fascinated me. I was dazzled by the colorful flower beds with their shiny white rocks. Every day as we walked or drove by, I would stare longingly, dreaming that I would one day own a house like that. Maybe I would own all of them. Why not? My father had instilled in me the power of possibility.

Panache Desai wrote in a blog post entitled *The Power of Possibility* that, "There comes a time when you feel the vibration of a new life awakening and expanding – when you have the burning desire to peek through a crack in your chrysalis and see the world and its possibilities in a whole new light. That desire is your soul signature – your true expression in the world – longing to spread its wings and break free. It's the voice inside that tells you that all you've ever wanted can be yours" (Desai, 2014).

Every time I saw those beautiful homes my world opened up a little bit more. I imagined how each house would be laid out on the inside and who would live in them. I visualized owning a row of homes in an upscale neighborhood. I saw children riding their bicycles up and down the street like I'd seen in the movies. I wasn't afraid to dream beyond what I knew. As far as I was concerned, nothing was impossible.

I was nine years old when I began my first entrepreneurial venture. Seeing my school mates had more than the basics, I naturally developed a hunger for some of those material things too. Fiercely independent, I didn't want to ask my parents for money. I wanted to make my own so that I could buy whatever I felt I needed.

My parents gave us kids an allowance of $20.00 a month. I daydreamed all the time about how I would make more money and how I could stretch what I had to get more. There were so many things that I wanted to buy such as a new bike or a skateboard. One day I came up with a bright idea. I took my allowance and walked down to the Circle K gas station around the corner from our home, where I bought a pack of 24 sticks of gum for $1.25. I went back home and sold each stick of gum for $.25 cents each to the children in my neighborhood, making a total of $6.00 with a profit of $4.75 from one pack of gum. That was a whopping 380% return on my investment. I was thrilled. So thrilled I felt compelled to go back and do it again and again. Eventually, my customer base of neighborhood children who couldn't afford to continually buy my product, dried up. All the same, I had made a total of $18.00 with a profit of $14.25 on my small investment of $3.75.

The power of imagination is more important than knowledge. Imagination is the catalyst behind every invention on the planet. The power of imagination is the power of possibility. And so for me, daydreaming was productive. I used that time to manifest in my mind's eye what it would be like to live in an upscale neighborhood. I visualized how it would feel to ride my bicycle to different parts of town. I formed dozens of mental images about how I would help my family and community, and what kind of lifestyle I would have. I loved to read because in my imagination I could travel anywhere in the world; there was no limitation on time or space. I could walk through walls if I wanted to.

Although children tend to have very vivid imaginations, daydreaming is encouraged less and less as we mature. Because of this, it becomes harder to believe in our dreams. Instead, we are told to pay more attention to more mundane things like our jobs, the bills, and climbing the corporate ladder. There is no time for imagination to freewheel by the time we are adults. Children, however, perfect the practice.

As a child, I had imagined I could do more with my allowance than just spend it on candy. I had learned a great work ethic from my parents, and imagination came naturally to me. I could see things as they were going to be before they ever came into fruition. I envisioned a life of financial freedom long before it ever happened. I saw my little chewing gum enterprise reaping a harvest of funds. At nine years old I had discovered how exciting it is to use your imagination with a little hard work to see an immediate return on an investment. This youthful experiment turned out to be the seed of greater things to come.

Imagination is therefore a powerful tool in the arsenal of possibility. A healthy imagination makes you more creative, resourceful, and productive. The use of imagination has proven physical and psychological benefits. It "provides temporary happiness, calmness and relief from stress. It can make you feel free, though temporarily, and only in the mind, from tasks, difficulties and unpleasant circumstances … Lack of understanding of the power of the imagination is responsible for the suffering, incompetence, difficulties, failures and unhappiness people experience" (Sasson, 2022).

Lessons on Love and Money

In sixth grade, my friend Jennifer came to school one day with a Walkman. My parents couldn't afford such luxuries and seeing hers caused me to long for the same thing. I asked Jennifer to walk home with me so that I could show the Walkman to my parents in the hope that they would buy me one. I hope to convince them that buying one for me was a good investment. I had been saving but I still didn't have enough. I pleaded with them to buy me one, but they said no and wouldn't relent.

I was enraged. I had counted on their approval and was disappointed and maybe a little embarrassed. I lost my temper and accused them of not loving me. Of course, I didn't understand anything about finances. I thought if they truly loved me, they would give me everything I asked for, whether I needed it or not. I was not able to discern the difference between need and want. I was clueless when it came to the economy of life. I knew that my parents provided what we needed and not much more — but I wanted more.

But the solution was there — in my mind. I knew from my prior experience that selling gum worked. I just needed to add another income stream. My grandmother and I collected aluminum cans and took them in for recycling. We got a nickel for every can. I didn't have to invest any money to pick up the cans and it wasn't long before I was able to buy my Walkman.

From my past chewing gum business, I learned how to work hard and be creative to make money. What was much harder for me to accept was the idea of cooperative economics, that is, pooling our resources for the greater good. I was so independent that I resented the idea of interdependence. I wanted to do everything on my own. I didn't want to have to ask permission or depend on anybody. I hadn't really internalized the lesson that loving support was also crucial to success. I resented my parents' struggle without seeing that they were willing to work as hard as they did because of the overwhelming love they had for each other, and for me and my siblings. I misinterpreted their diligence and hard work as something negative when, in fact, it was one of the most positive lessons they taught me.

However, there is a false narrative that you have to be married with children to find true happiness. This portrayal of marriage and children as the ultimate arrangement is a by-product of patriarchal societies. The idea that you have to fall madly in love with your soul mate to find joy is also a falsehood. If you are not happy with yourself, then depending upon another person for your happiness is only going to serve as a temporary fix. The myth of a single soul somewhere in the universe who will make you complete leads so much disenchantment. There are so many more ways to experience true love than a romantic connection.

If you want to be happy, fall madly in love with life. You can find joy in your daily pursuits. Happiness is not contingent upon whether or not you have a partner, a spouse, children, or lots of money in the bank. Love is the greatest gift you can give or receive, including giving it to yourself. Whether it be with relatives or strangers, when we transfer loving energy, we empower one another by adding a sense of joy and peace to one another. Love alone does not guarantee you financial success or stability, but it will help you get through the rough patches.

Money also has its place. It connects you to the resources you need to help yourself and others. You cannot pour from an empty cup. If your heart's desire is to give to those in need, build houses for the poor, or start a non-profit organization that reaches the world, you need finances. If you just want to take care of yourself and your family, you need money. It's very difficult to give anything when you can't take care of yourself.

When put in perspective, there is an extremely bigger payoff on investment if you include love and happiness in the mix. Financial abundance without love and happiness can make you miserable. Love without money can have the same effect. You can have both if you learn the art of balance and some necessary building blocks.

Building Blocks

As you can see, I was born with an independent spirit and a mind of my own. I was rarely swayed by other people's opinions or influence. The building blocks of my life started with a stubborn will that never quit. Because I am a dreamer I continually built on my creativity, the plethora of ideas that would come to me often awake or in my sleep about what I could do to build my empire. I was blessed with a family that loved, cared for, and supported me even when I did something that went beyond the bounds of my culture and upbringing.

I had learned how to think like a businesswoman from my chewing gum venture. I learned about basic customer service, supply and demand, and marketing. Of course, at nine years old I didn't recognize these abstract principles. There were, however, other components needed for me to be able to build the business I dreamed of. I had yet to learn, for instance, that success without love, joy, and peace of mind was really not success at all.

I've always been driven. Once I set my mind on something, it was a done deal. I tenaciously pursued whatever it was that I wanted, no matter the consequences. This did not always work to my advantage. Tenacity turned inside out is also a synonym for stubbornness. Your biggest strength can also be your greatest weakness. Though I appreciated my parents' hard work, I vowed to myself that I would do something different. I would make them proud. I would make a way for them and for me to not ever again work as hard as they did to provide us with the bare necessities. I knew from my little ventures that one day I would own a business that would help me to take care of myself and my family. I continued to build on this knowledge as I grew older.

It would be many years before I came to the fullness of the knowledge concerning the building blocks I needed for a successful, happy life. All I was focused on at nine years old was making money to buy the things that ambitious, precocious kids long for. I used my imagination to its fullest extent to achieve my goals.

CHAPTER FOUR

DREAM KILLERS

At the age of twelve, it took me some time to realize that other Hmong girls my age were not out playing as much as I was. I was old enough to help with the cooking and cleaning, but my mom and my grandma usually took care of all that. Occasionally, I was tasked with babysitting my siblings and helping with clearing and cleaning the dishes. But the boys were the ones who spent most of their day outside playing. It appeared that every time I would ask the girls to come out and play, they were either cleaning or helping to cook in the kitchen. Over time, some Hmong parents stopped allowing their daughters to hang out with me, saying I was lazy and a bad influence because I didn't cook and clean like most Hmong girls.

My mother, being a traditional Hmong housewife, didn't work outside the home except for the garden. She was submissive to her husband, and she served her family well. She couldn't drive or speak any English. Where was the time for all that with seven children? It seemed to me that it was ingrained in her head that women and girls couldn't do anything more than housework and having babies. A traditional Hmong female wouldn't so much as shake hands with a stranger, especially a man. Traditionally, the father is primarily responsible for financial support and making decisions for the family. Mothers are responsible for emotional support and taking care of the children.

As for me, I did not want my life to be ruled like that. I loved my mother, but I vowed I would never be any man's servant. That's what marriage looked like to me. I wanted an equal partnership with my mate, not to be confined to what I saw as slave labor. Many Asian men were brought up to be the unquestioned heads of the household. Their word was absolute. I wasn't the kind of person who took crap from anyone. I couldn't see myself quietly obeying another human being or being subservient to a man's needs. I certainly wasn't going to let a man keep me from pursuing my dream. I had made up my mind that I was going to be a CEO one day and nobody was going to keep me from it. Not tradition, not family, and certainly not the bonds of marriage.

Thinking the way I did made me a bit of an outcast. In accordance with old Hmong customs, many girls weren't allowed to work or get a higher education and, even among Hmong in America, these rules didn't vary much. Boys were treated with reverence and respect; girls were only useful as potential mothers and homemakers. It was a long time before women and girls would begin to break those rules and smash the old molds. Many women have had to fight with family and community to get an education, gain employment, play sports, and interact with men in any capacity outside of the home.

Hmong girls were told, "You shall not get pregnant out of wedlock, shame the family, speak back; you must obey your in-laws and your husband" (Wozniacka, 2012). Hmong American women struggle daily with the divide between cultures, often having to balance or take sides concerning what they should do in any given circumstance.

America was a place of transition for Hmong men too. From being used to having complete control over their households, they too struggled with the culture shock they faced in America. "In Laos, whatever the man says goes. In this country, all of a sudden, the tables have turned. It's like a storm that's raging all the time and the men have to find the calmness within it" (Wozniacka, 2012). Some men managed to find the balance; others resorted to anger, drinking, and abuse.

Many parents fear that their children will lose respect for their culture, so they lament the changes that are associated with western society. Parents, caught between the old and the new order, try their best to maintain the cultural standard. If the way the other girls' parents treated me was any indication of how I would be accepted as a CEO, then I had to brace myself for a long, hard road.

Authority Figures

When I was in the eighth grade, my parents found a house across town. I was extremely excited to move. Our big family was finally leaving a life of cramped apartments. My father had worked hard and kept his promise that we would live in a beautiful big house in America like the people in the movies. He had made that dream come true. I was absolutely ecstatic! For me, it demonstrated that no matter where you've come from, anything is possible if you believe. I didn't even mind that I would have to attend a new school and make new friends. I wasn't the least bit nervous about meeting new people. Making friends came pretty easily to me and I looked forward to the next stage of our family's adventure.

I met Janice and Gloria in eighth grade. They quickly became my new best friends, and we stayed friends through my ninth grade year of high school. We all shared the same passion for school and our future goals. We were young, but we were devoted to our educational pursuits and professional aspirations. Our parents were strict, so we didn't go out much after school. Even so, I may have snuck out a few times here and there to hang out with my friends. Back then, we didn't have social media or cell phones to take pictures with our friends. We used disposable cameras, which required us to bring them in to get prints made, so there were times when it took weeks before we could even look at the images. Our idea of a good time was going to One-Hour Photo Studios to take pictures to share with one another and sometimes hanging out at the library for hours.

I've always loved learning and enjoyed the challenge of completing a tough assignment. I was curious about everything. In the ninth grade, when presented with the task of choosing a career and doing a presentation about how we were going to accomplish our goals after high school, I was thrilled. I was going to be the Chief Executive Officer of my own company. I created a detailed business plan with charts and tables. It took a lot of time and research. I couldn't wait to share all the information with my class. Everybody else talked about being doctors, teachers, lawyers, and even an astronaut. My English teacher seemed to enjoy all of their presentations and I couldn't wait to share mine.

Finally, it was my turn. I talked about what it meant to be a CEO, the name of my company, and its mission statement. I discussed growth and development. I threw in some tidbits about sales and marketing. I was proud of myself because I had put in a lot of work and, truth be told, I never got a grade lower than a 'B.'

My teacher, however, was not impressed at all. To my dismay, she looked at me, shook her head, and told me that building my own business and becoming a CEO was not a career. She promptly gave me a 'D' on the assignment. I was devastated. Getting good grades fueled my dreams, dreams which were strongly connected to my self-image. I felt like my teacher wasn't just attacking my dream; she was also attacking me personally and I didn't measure up. In my young mind, there was something wrong with me. Maybe the kids who teased me were right. Maybe I wasn't as pretty, as talented, as capable, as smart as they were. Some kids were really mean.

That day I believed my teacher. After all, she was an authority figure, not one of the kids on the playground. She was an adult, and I was a child. She had gone to college; I was just starting high school. Maybe she knew a few things that I didn't. She was born and raised an American. She knew the rules. I had only been in the States a few years. What did

I know? She brought my foundation down to the dust. She convinced me that my lifelong dream was impossible. I began doubting myself. I didn't want to go to English class anymore. I was embarrassed and ashamed. My father had made the American dream a possibility, but this American teacher had snatched my dream away from me and torn it to shreds.

Dreams Deferred

In his poem *Dream Deferred* (Langston Hughes, 1967/1992) wrote:

What happens to a dream deferred?
Does it dry up like a raisin in the sun?
Or fester like a sore – And then run?
Does it stink like rotten meat?
Or crust and sugar over – Like a syrupy sweet?
Maybe it just sags like a heavy load.
Or does it explode?

We all know that having a vision for what you want helps you to focus on and achieve your goals. Without a vision you can be easily distracted and disenchanted. My hopes were crushed by my teacher's negative assessment. I didn't want to go to English class anymore. Since our school was an open campus, students were able to go in and out of school whenever they wanted. So instead of going to class the next day, I sat outside on a bench staring out into the parking lot depressed and terribly discouraged.

Several students attended the college across the street. My girlfriends and I had talked about going there and attending classes too. I stared across that parking lot, feeling lost and disoriented. I was unsure of what I wanted anymore. I had lost all clarity on my dreams and aspirations. Did what I wanted make any difference anyway? Many of the young girls with whom I went to school were already married and had children. Some of them never returned to school after the wedding.

I asked myself why I had allowed myself to be so offended by just one teacher's assessment. After all, was I not the adventurous, unconventional one? Did I not have enough confidence in my own convictions to override her report?

Apparently not. In some mysterious way I had internalized the concept of authority figures. Maybe it's because I had a high regard for school and the entire learning environment. I could not explain it at the time but as I grew older, I studied the phenomenon deeper. For most people, teachers, doctors, lawyers are all people we believe in by virtue of their authority. We believe that because they have a particular education or insight, their judgment must be infallible and true.

One experiment brought this home to me. Conducted in the 1960s by Yale psychologist Dr. Stanley Milgram, it concerned people's unquestioning regard for those in authority. Milgram was attempting to understand why the Germans succumbed to Nazi authority even when their conscience told them it was wrong.

The experiment consisted of three people — a participant (called the teacher), an actor (called the learner), and the scientist. The participant was to deliver an electric shock to the person on the other side of the door when he answered questions incorrectly. The participant did not know the learner was an actor who was complicit in the experiment and wasn't actually getting shocked. Two thirds of the people who were participants or teachers (65%), administered up to the highest degree of shock — 450 volts — enough to kill a man, in compliance with authority. All participants went up to at least 300 volts (Cherry, 2019).

What scientists learned from Milgram's hugely unethical experiments and subsequent experiments by other scientists was that "the physical presence of an authority figure can dramatically increase compliance" (Cherry, 2019). If this happens in the confines of an established institution like a school or hospital, the effect is multiplied. People tend to believe and obey those they trust in positions of power, sometimes even when their conscience and intuition tell them something different.

The sad truth is that just because someone says something is right or true, doesn't necessarily mean it is so. Just because somebody has a degree doesn't mean they know it all. I wish I understood that when I was growing up. Just because someone is an authority doesn't mean you have to take their word for it.

In my case, in a single moment of time, one teacher had clouded the landscape of possibility for me and snatched away my dreams. I was young and still relatively new to the American way of life. I didn't know the rules here. I trusted her guidance. For the first time in my young life, her words had imploded my hope of a career and a better future. I sat on that bench feeling robbed, assaulted, insulted – and ashamed.

As I sat in that parking lot so disoriented, a girl from one of my classes sat down and said hello. Although we had talked in class a few times, we weren't friends and had never hung out before. With Janice and Gloria, I didn't need any other friends. But that day was different. This girl invited me to a barbecue to hang out with her and some friends. She said her boyfriend had just gotten out of jail. I didn't bother to ask what he had gone to jail for. I didn't need to know the details. I needed an escape. She was offering one and I took it. In my mind, it was less humiliating than going to English class, so I skipped the rest of the school day.

I thoroughly enjoyed the barbecue, mostly because I didn't have to think or feel. All I wanted to do was have a good time. The next day, my classmate and I met up again with a few more of her friends and poked around the mall. Another day, we went to the pool hall. Eventually, I met some of her other friends from other schools. Together, we would often skip school to spend time socializing at their houses. There were weeks where I went to school for a day and other times where I didn't bother going at all. They smoked and drank, and though I didn't do either of these things with them, I was guilty by association. Their lifestyle became the norm for me. I didn't care about anything anymore.

My best friends, Janice and Gloria, eclipsed into the shadows. They were no longer as interesting or as cool as the new crew. Going to the library and talking about dreams that would never happen was pointless. We became distant and I spent less and less time with them. They both eventually moved away, and I never heard from them again.

Of course, my parents weren't happy about the changes they saw in me. They didn't understand and I didn't tell them. I was too mortified. I could not bring myself to share the indignity of receiving such a low grade. My parents didn't yell. They nagged. In response I threatened to run away and never come back if they didn't stop bothering me about school. They were as worried, and probably as confused as I was.

The more my parents scolded and tried to discipline me, the angrier and more distant I became. True to my word, I ran off and stayed away for five days. Even though I was staying at a friend's house, they had no idea where I was. When I came home, the cycle of nagging and reprimanding started again. This time I took off for an entire week leaving my parents completely in the dark concerning my whereabouts.

There is no greater fear for a parent than for their child to disappear into thin air, especially an immigrant female child. My parents were sick with worry, not knowing whether I was dead or alive. I was spiraling out and there was nothing they could do to stop it.

I had lost my sense of purpose. Up to the day of that ninth grade presentation, I had no doubt that I would own and build an empire one day. The teacher's comments and low grade left me feeling guilty. Had I dishonored myself and my family? Why did I feel so sad and alone? Why was I spending so much time with people who didn't want or expect anything more out of life? What was happening to the girl who always wanted more?

In Asian families, interdependence is the knot that ties us together. It is how refugee families were able to function and stay alive before and after the

Vietnam war. If you had no family, you had no support. If you in any way brought dishonor to yourself, you automatically dishonored your family as you were not seen as separate from them but a part of the whole. Individualism and 'self-esteem' were primarily western ideals where emphasis is placed on individual achievement. Material wealth, status, and self-mastery are the hallmarks of achievement. As a product of two cultures, I had become lost on my road to success and ended up taking several detours and wrong turns into winding, unchartered territory.

Believing the negative messages from people in authority, I started doubting all of my abilities. I felt hopeless and helpless. My dream that I had held onto for dear life had become irrelevant based upon the word of someone else. Now all of the negative messaging from my culture began to pile on. "Nobody is going to want to marry you. You're not good enough. Being a CEO is not a career. You can't cook. You can't do anything right. You're lazy." Gone was the childhood belief in myself. Here was I, a teenager still going through all the changes of puberty and trying to figure out who I was. In my mind, everybody was essentially telling me I was nothing. The dreams and ideas I had spent years fantasizing about were meaningless.

These people were my authority figures, and I had no reason to believe that they were telling me a lie. Even if some of them never meant to hurt me, the damage had been done. My self-esteem was effectively shattered.

My father decided on a new plan to rein in my behavior. He thought I needed a change to interrupt the pattern I had chosen. Figuring that it was my new friends that had caused me to adopt this volatile behavior, he decided the best thing to do was to keep me away from them. The only way to do that was to send me to my uncle in Minnesota. His plan was designed to give me a fresh start. I didn't fight him on it, but I felt abandoned.

My parents didn't yell at me — they weren't mad. They were sad, disappointed, and afraid. Their ambitious, inquisitive little girl had become someone else in such a short period of time it made their heads spin. They didn't know how broken I was or the reason why. They couldn't have possibly comprehended the extent of that brokenness because I was too ashamed to tell them. My behavior was a symptom of a much deeper problem.

When your self-esteem is eroded, there are certain psychological effects that come into play. When you feel bad about yourself, you tend to take that out on other people, usually the ones closest to you. In close families, you take it out on one another creating a concentric circle of unproductive behaviors. When the root cause isn't addressed in any situation, the problem is compounded.

My dad bought me a plane ticket and I flew to my uncle's. I didn't put up a fight. I was obedient in whatever my parents felt was best. I knew going away wasn't the answer, but I had no solution. I still didn't want to go to school because I had developed a fear of failure and that fear was crippling me.

As usual, it took no time at all for me to make new friends at my uncle's. Unfortunately, I chose to surround myself with the same kinds of friends I had left behind. They drank, smoked, cursed, and fought. They didn't go to school and neither did I. Yeah, I had other friends that were all about education and going to college, but they weren't any fun. I gravitated instead to those who were just as broken inside as I was. Misery loves company, right? And I had plenty of it.

A change in environment hadn't changed the sadness in my heart. Being homesick was an additional weight. I was angry with the world. There was no distance that could have alleviated that. It wasn't long before my family realized things weren't working out. I packed my things again, boarded a bus, and headed back home to sunny California.

I somehow managed to pass my freshman year. Researchers say freshman year at any school including middle school, high school, and college is the most demanding and frustrating of any of the years following. The transition from middle school to high school can be challenging when puberty kicks in, hormones are out of control, and young people are facing an identity crisis. Class structure is different. There are more teachers, more classes, and more assignments to remember. Friends you knew in middle school may have become someone else in the process of trying to navigate popularity, grades, and relationships. I had excelled throughout my academic career until that day when I had allowed one teacher to throw me so far off course. I never knew if I could find my way back.

On my return to California, I was enrolled in the same school I had been in previously. I sought out the same group of friends I had left behind. My mother, in her concern about my education and my behavior, would visit the school often to check up on me and speak to the school counselor. Her goal was to work with the school counselor to develop an academic plan to get me back on track. In order to achieve that, she shared a great deal of personal information about what was happening with me outside of the classroom. Since she doesn't speak any English, an interpreter was provided for her and the many other Hmong parents in the community. The interpreter was not discreet. He shared my personal problems with the parents of the other Hmong students. These parents then warned their children not to associate with me, leaving me feeling even more isolated.

I've never done drugs or gotten into a fist fight. I had an altercation with a girl once. As a result, her parents immediately had her taken out of school. Within 24 hours she was transferred somewhere else. I never saw her again. I wondered if that was my fault because I was labeled by the company I kept.

Sophomore year was a breeze compared to my first year in high school. It flew by. Threatened with summer school if I didn't pass all of my classes, I buckled down a little. I certainly wasn't about to let school ruin my summer fun. I knew I didn't need an 'A' to pass so I scratched through the bare minimum in every class. I was smart so it didn't take much to manipulate the educational system to my advantage. I was promoted to the eleventh grade.

That summer I met the man who would later become my husband.

Facing Reality

At the start of my junior year, I was enrolled in an occupational class. Going on actual job interviews at local banks and businesses was part of the course requirements. The goal was to obtain employment and maintain it. That's the only way you could earn credits to pass the course. I hated the entire process. My last interview was at the headquarters of a juvenile detention center. I got the job. Working with the counselors in the detention center was like living an episode of the old television show *Scared Straight.*

All youth detention centers in California are operated and run by the California Department of Corrections and Rehabilitation, Division of Juvenile Justice. Young people under the age of 18 can be held at a detention center for up to 30 days depending on the severity of the offense. They are ordered there by a judge and the check-in process is similar to that of adult criminals. The most common juvenile offenses are theft and assault. Other popular criminal offenses among juveniles in the state of California are illegal drug possession and sales. The center where I worked housed some of the more heinous offenders. Counselors would tell me stories of the horrendous acts perpetrated by these young people, many of whom were my age. They also shared the devastating stories of some of their deaths.

Life in a youth detention center didn't seem like it was an easy one. Most facilities are pretty old, usually former prisons with cells and dorms with narrow rows of bunks. A typical day starts between 6:00 and 7:00 in the morning. The young people are grouped together and taken through various tasks throughout the day under adult and guard supervision. But the guards don't see everything. Just as in adult prisons, some guards are guilty of criminal activity against these young prisoners. The idea of grouping troubled youths together with others who have issues and are exhibiting criminal behavior is often a set-up for more criminal activity even when there are support programs in place.

After many days of listening to the counselors talk, and witnessing young people who looked like me, I realized a common theme. They were no different from the kids I had chosen to hang around with. Was I choosing to become like that? I was already guilty by association. What if I ended up in a place like that? What if something were to happen to me? How would my parents feel if I died? I began to question my life choices. I was the oldest. I was supposed to be the most responsible. Who would take care of my siblings and protect my parents in their old age? I was blessed to have parents who loved, cared and provided for me. What was I doing to myself? To my family?

The more stories I heard, the more it made me think. I was reminded of the little girl in the refugee camp peeking in windows to learn how to master the ABC and English words. I remembered how badly I yearned to go to school and my joy at the thought of my first day. Not even being laughed at could have dissuaded me from that excitement. What had happened to the dreamer? Would my dreams die with me as some of those young people had died? Did they once have dreams too?

I realized what a great opportunity I had been given. I was suddenly very grateful for my family, their work ethic, and the vision they had instilled in me. It's true the dreamer had lost her way and taken a detour, but she was back and ready to once again pursue her dream. I stopped skipping classes and started focusing on school. I knew I needed to do better. I changed my attitude, my friends, and my outlook. I focused on my future.

Ty, a boy I met at a get-together hosted by one of my friends, was becoming a big part of that future. Before we were introduced, a friend of mine said Ty looked like a gangster. He did, in fact, have a bit of a criminal history. He was the epitome of a bad boy complete with the machismo image. That wasn't really my type. I didn't know him, neither was I interested in talking to him. I didn't think the two of us would have anything to talk about. Besides that, I was already in love with someone else.

Several weeks later, Ty called me out of the blue. I didn't know where he had gotten my number. Turns out, someone at the party had shared it with him. I refused to talk to him at first, but Ty was persistent. He kept calling, asking if he could come hang out with me. Finally, I agreed. When he came, we sat out front of my house and talked for hours. I was surprised at how much we actually had in common. We were both big dreamers. This was the initial attraction. We talked about travel and all the places we wanted to see, the things we would accomplish, and how grand an adventure our lives would be. We even discussed what we would want in a future partner.

He came to visit regularly after that. Not every day but often enough to spark my interest. We didn't actually date. We spent most of our time sitting outside my house and talking. I didn't meet his parents or get to know his friends. We didn't go to the movies, or to dances. We just became good friends. Then he asked me to marry him. He promised me that he would work really hard and give me the world. He promised me a good life. The first time he asked, I let him know that I wasn't ready for marriage. I was going into my junior year of high school. In the back of my mind there was still the promise I had made to myself to be more than the traditional Hmong housewife having babies and taking care of a husband and home.

In the days and months to follow, we spent more and more time together. We were inseparable, seeing each other nearly every day. He asked me to marry him again. Over the course of the summer, we got to know each other on a much deeper level. I believed in him and the promises he made. I envisioned us building a great future together. I knew I was young, but my parents had gotten married young and they had done well. They may not have been in love at first, but they managed to build a good life together. My life would be a little different. Besides, some of my school friends were already married. A few already had children. I would get married too and my life would be complete. Unlike my parents, I would marry someone I loved who claimed to love me, someone I had chosen for myself instead of being arranged. We would be a powerful couple. I believed that side by side Ty and I could conquer the world.

So, at the age of 16, I left home one evening and married, in traditional Hmong fashion, my 21-year-old husband.

Old Traditions - New Beginnings

Hmong people are the few refugees who have managed to retain their ancient cultural practices amid American traditions. Child brides were seen as a necessary evil in a culture where the average lifespan was only thirty to forty years old. It was normal for girls as young as thirteen years old to be married off to much older men. Money was exchanged between families just as it was in the British dowry system. Bride capture was also the norm. Early marriage and childbearing helped offset a casualty rate of more than 100 times the US during the Vietnam war of the 1960s (Arax, 1993). Hmong men thus preferred young girls to women their own age. They have a saying, "If you marry a girl your age, by the time she has given you enough children, she will look twice your age" (Arax, 1993).

Many times, these marriage contracts were instituted against the girl's will. A particularly adamant bride-to-be would often try to run away before her arranged marriage. This would bring great dishonor to the family, and she could never return.

A Hmong marriage ceremony is a far cry from the traditional American wedding. The girl typically just packs her things, leaves her family sometime during the night, and goes to the home of her husband and his family. Before the bride can enter the house, an elder wave a live rooster over the heads of the bride and groom three times while chanting a verse to welcome the bride's spirit. The rooster is then let go alive as the couple silently enter the house. Once the door is closed, everyone inside can welcome the bride. She is then sent off to the bedroom while the groom kneels to thank his parents and ancestors for the blessing. The ceremony itself doesn't take very long. Another ceremony involving the couple's marriage agreement is usually held at a later date.

Ty told me he lived with his brother and sister-in-law, but I had never been to his house before we got married. His family lived on the other side of town and, quite frankly, I wasn't really interested in meeting anyone. This, too, wasn't unusual, in that most Hmong girls didn't meet their husband's family until the day they were married. Imagine my horror when, within a week, I learned that my husband had several children from a previous marriage, two of whom lived with him. He had conveniently omitted that bit of information throughout our entire courtship.

Overnight I became a 16-year-old stepmother. I realized too late that I had made a rash, spur-of-the-moment decision that I couldn't take back. I had not done my due diligence. I thought Ty was an honest man and I had no reason to suspect he would lie to me by omission.

I couldn't now run crying and screaming to my parents about how Ty had deceived me. I wondered what else he had lied to me about. What other things had he omitted? What else was there that I didn't know? I wasn't ready for motherhood. I could hardly take care of myself, much less two children whom I didn't know. The only thing I knew how to cook was rice. What was I going to feed them? Divorce is strictly taboo in my culture. I couldn't tarnish my name and my parents' reputation. Besides, my parents would disown me if I went back. Then where would I be?

All of this ran across my mind as I pondered my situation. Trapped and afraid was an understatement. What had I gotten myself into this time? This was totally out of line with the orderly plan I had for my life. My marriage was not at all what I had envisioned. I was about to be thrown straight into motherhood and housework. There would be no time for me to get acclimated. Caught between the proverbial rock and a hard place, I made up my mind to stay. Our real wedding wouldn't take place until after I graduated high school.

In the meantime, I worked at being the best wife and stepmother a 16-year-old child could be.

CHAPTER FIVE

MARRIAGE AND THE MONSTERS UNDER THE BED

I was terrified of what I had gotten myself into. Nevertheless, Ty and I made the best of the first year of our marriage. We shared chores, cooking and cleaning together as partners. We both took care of the children. Ty would come to my school during my lunch break, and we would share a meal together. We didn't have cell phones then, but we each had pagers. He would send me cute little messages throughout the day. When I was pregnant and had a craving, Ty didn't hesitate to go out and get me what I wanted, no matter the time of day or night. He was attentive and caring. He would come straight home every day after work to spend quality time with our little family. We were the perfect young newlyweds.

By the time I was a senior in high school, we had two children. This wasn't unusual for Hmong girls. I, at least, got to choose my husband. I knew many young girls my age whose husbands were chosen for them, were beaten and treated badly by their husbands. This, too, was not unusual. Ty didn't hit me when we argued. And we argued more frequently as time went on.

I don't know when things began to change. I cannot pinpoint the day but the closeness we shared evaporated into a cold aloofness. I don't know when or why we stopped sharing and talking about our dreams. It may have happened by degrees, but all of a sudden cooking became my sole responsibility. Ty stopped helping around the house and in the kitchen. Every day after work he would come home with a case of beer, sit around, and drink. He began coming home at two in the morning, claiming he was working late. He worked later and later hours, extending more and more into the next day. It got to the point that he wasn't coming home at all. When he was home, he was often drunk and belligerent.

Because Ty didn't hit me, I thought I was lucky. There were plenty of women who suffered much worse. Ty only yelled and called me names. Though he made me feel small, unloved, and insignificant, at least he never struck me. I gave him points for that. I didn't know any better.

The top risk factors for abuse in the Asian community are strict patriarchal leadership and gender roles. Women and girls raised in communities that still adhere to child marriage traditions — even though they are considered illegal in the United States — face a particularly difficult choice. If they balk the system, they can be ostracized from their clan and family, the very structure that helps them to survive. Independent women can be intimidating in a culture that values interdependence and male leadership. I admit I wasn't timid in the least. I was never afraid to speak my mind in an argument. I could be formidable in a fight. But I was also a wife who desperately tried to please her husband and get our marriage back on track.

However, no matter how hard I tried, I couldn't make Ty the happy, romantic partner I had known. I had gone straight to work full-time after I graduated high school. We were a family of six — his two children from a previous marriage, our two children, and the two of us — living in a cramped, one bedroom apartment. We were both making $6.00 an hour at our respective jobs. He owed a great deal in child support and his income wasn't nearly enough to keep up with that. I thought if I could contribute more, maybe he would be less stressed. Taking care of a new wife, an estranged wife, and raising a family was expensive. Maybe if I helped out more he wouldn't be so angry. We could be partners again like we vowed to one another in the days we sat outside my parents' house talking.

I decided to take another income route and get into retail sales. Every couple of weeks Ty and I would drive down to Los Angeles and buy a truckload of products to sell at Denio's flea market. I enlisted my siblings to help. We were all at Denio's every weekend hustling to make sales. Some days we would make as much as $500 to $600. Other days we might only make $80. Although we were working for ourselves, we still weren't making enough money for me to quit my full time job. I was hoping I could make things better, but instead they were becoming progressively worse.

Marriage is a two-way street. Sometimes you will have to give 60% while your spouse gives 40%. Some days your spouse will work at things ten times harder than you. There are no guarantees because you are two individuals trying to mesh your personalities, foibles, and flaws into one cohesive unit. It isn't easy for two people to become one, especially if they start with different foundations. You both can get lost in the dynamics of trying to piece everything together. It is soul-destroying to watch it all fall apart.

I tried to figure out why Ty drank so much. I thought of ways to ease the struggle he was apparently dealing with. Like a good wife, I wanted to be his support, but the drinking and disappearances continued. As a result, so did our fighting. He hurled spiteful words and whatever objects he could get his hands on in the moment. I countered with a few choice words of my own. I thought often about packing up our two kids and leaving; but the weight of dishonor that would be heaped on my family was too much for me to bear.

Divorce was still not an option. I kept telling myself things would get better. After all, he hadn't laid a hand on me, so I reasoned that I could have been overreacting. I wasn't in the hospital with a concussion. I wasn't dead. My feelings were just hurt. I tricked myself into believing that his verbal abuse was no big deal. The truth of the matter was that our once happy home had become a battlefield. I spent almost every night crying alone. This wasn't the life I had envisioned for us. I longed for the man who had promised me the world. What had happened to him? Where had he gone?

Most men are raised with a qualifier: to provide for themselves and their family, no excuses. What happens when they can't do that? How are they affected when opportunities are closed to them? What happens when resources to help them improve and move forward are not available? Are they allowed to cry about it? In most cultures they aren't even given the right to express what they feel. The more a culture is governed by the expectation of male dominance, the more the problems. I don't know what was going through my husband's mind. I couldn't speak for him or understand the pain because he would not share with me. Like my parents who were at a loss when I wouldn't go to school and kept running away, I was at a loss too. More often than not, I blamed myself. He blamed me too. Everything blurred in the face of the grief we both were feeling.

The night before our formal wedding, Ty went out with his friends. At midnight he was still not home. I had asked him not to go out so that he and I could spend time together with his family preparing for the next day's ceremony. He ignored me and left, leaving me feeling awkward and alone with his relatives.

As I lay in bed that night, I felt irrepressibly sad. Tears streaked my face and spread onto my pillow. Regret flooded my being. What had I done? What had I gotten myself into? Was this how it was going to be forever? Would it get better or were we just going through a phase? There has got to be more to marriage than this lonely, empty feeling. I felt trapped.

Ty finally came home at 1:00 in the morning, drunk as usual and hostile. I asked, "Where have you been?" He ignored me.

"Why did you go out the night before our wedding?"

His eyes bore through me like a slap in the face. "Why do you feel the need to control me?" His voice was mounting. He started yelling and calling me names. The ruckus was so loud, his parents knocked on the bedroom door. Without waiting for a response, his father stepped in.

Concerned, he asked, "What's going on in here?"

"Mind your own business!" Ty yelled louder, totally disrespecting his father. Then his eyes fell on Chao, the Mej Koob (pronounced May Kong) he had invited to negotiate the terms of the marriage.

"Why is he here this late at night?"

Ty turned and glared at me. In his drunkenness he had forgotten that he had been the one to pick up Chao earlier that day. He had decided that Chao would be instrumental in helping to prepare for the wedding. It was he who had orchestrated the sleeping arrangements.

Ty walked towards me, his eyes penetrating. He grabbed my arm, squeezing it hard. "You slept with him, didn't you? You whore!"

For the first time, I thought he might hit me. Alarm bells of terror set off in my head. Before I knew it, the men in the room reached out quickly and grabbed Ty, yanking him away from me, keeping him from doing any further harm.

"What are you talking about?" I cried, confused as to why he would attack me the way he did. Why would he make such accusations?

In answer, he picked up one of my high-heeled shoes and threw it across the room with the precision and force of an inebriated baseball player. The heel of the shoe hit the television screen so hard the screen shattered. I felt just as shattered.

I screamed at him, hot tears staining my cheeks. "Did you forget tomorrow is our wedding? You didn't even stay home and help me! I was here all day getting ready and how dare you come home and say that to me!"

He pointed a contemptuous finger in my direction. "I know there is someone else in your head. Who is he?"

He walked closer, shoving me against the wall, his accusing finger jabbing my forehead. I looked away, tears rolling down my face. How could this be happening to me?

Then, all of a sudden, he pulled me to him and hugged me. "I'm sorry," he said. He tried to kiss me as if nothing had ever happened. I looked away. His breath reeked of alcohol! My body shook with fear. I needed to create distance between us, so I disentangled myself, walked to the bathroom, and locked the door behind me. I spent the night before our wedding sleeping on the bathroom floor.

We arrived at my parent's house the next day at a little past noon. Ty's brother Nathan drove us in a van with Chao, Ty's best man Simon, and my bridesmaid Candy.

In an American wedding the bridesmaids are chosen by the bride and their responsibilities are to provide emotional support throughout the wedding planning and ceremony. In a traditional Hmong wedding, there is only one bridesmaid, and she is chosen by the groom's family. The main and only reason for that was to make sure that the bride does not run off to be with another man. This stemmed from years ago when brides would try to run off with a lover from another nearby village rather than be forced into a loveless marriage. Some girls would even jump off a cliff with the man they loved, believing that the only way they could be together was in spirit, reborn in another life and able to start anew.

All of the relatives on both sides of our family had already gathered outside my parents' home waiting for us. The two car garage was packed with people preparing for the feast that would follow the wedding ceremony. The sight of it all made me sick.

Nathan parked the van in front of the garage, and we all climbed out. A few of my male cousins pulled up beside us. They parked their small car on the other side of the road. Each of them carried a case of beer with them as they got out. I cringed at the thought of more alcohol. The events of the night before were still fresh in my mind. I shuddered at the thought of Ty getting brutally drunk again on our wedding day.

I can still run away, I thought to myself. *Do I really want to go through with this? I should just take my kids and run, maybe move across the country. I could go to New York and live my life far away from everyone. My love has waned. Aren't married people supposed to love one another?* Those are the questions I asked myself. Ty loved alcohol and partying so much more than he loved me — if he loved me at all.

Being a dutiful daughter can be a great responsibility to bear. If I grabbed my children, hiked up my skirts, and ran like hell, my parents would lose face in front of the entire community. They had worked so hard to get to the place where they were in life. I couldn't bring shame upon them. It didn't matter that I no longer loved my husband. I had a duty to fulfill to my family, my children. What I truly wanted didn't matter in the face of that burden. I set aside my personal needs and desires for what I thought was the greater good. I was willing to live with the repercussions of that — at least for the time being.

The marriage ceremony was a blur. I had zoned out from the first words to the farewell. When it was time for us to leave, my father's sister told me, "Don't look back." My mom admonished me to "Be a good daughter-in-law so that they will love you." I smiled through tears.

We piled back into the van. As it took off, I did look back. Life as I had known it was over. I could no longer fall back into the bosom of my family. I couldn't cry to my mother or expect my father to take me back into the safety of my childhood home. I cried earnest tears not knowing what else life was going to throw at me. Would the abuse continue? How was I going to protect my children? Myself?

According to the Asian Pacific Institute on Gender Based Violence, up to 55% of women in Asian American communities suffer from domestic violence. And these are the cases that are reported. Some researchers say this number can be as high as 70%. Husbands expect their wives to be submissive in all things, never to talk back or question decisions or choices. I chose to stay with my husband even as the abuse escalated for the sake of my children. I wanted them to have a stable home with both parents. That's what I knew growing up. I withstood the abuse and the shame for their sakes. We act upon what we know in any given situation, and I thought staying and trying to work through things was the best possible solution.

Murphy's law states that anything that can go wrong will, and at the worst possible moment. As if things weren't bad enough, a few weeks after our wedding our apartment caught on fire, forcing us to move. We rented an old three bedroom house and, though it was a step up from the one bedroom apartment, it was also more expensive and beyond our budget. One advantage was that the house was in a part of town that was far away from Ty's friends. This meant he wasn't linking up with them and going out nearly as much.

We still weren't making enough to support ourselves and our family. There were times when we couldn't pay our rent or buy enough food. We had a better place to live but we weren't living any better. This must have discouraged Ty. He started drinking and going out again, coming home in a stupor in the middle of the night. His appearances were becoming more and more infrequent. When he was home, we argued and fought. It was a concentric circle of disappearances, arguments, and him slamming the door behind him. Was this what other marriages were like? I felt like a single parent raising our children alone.

Our retail business lasted a year before we called it quits. Even though I enjoyed the freedom of working for myself, it took too much time and effort with very little returns. Secretly I had hoped the work would keep Ty busy and at home more often. He was excited at first and helped a lot. Always a dreamer, I kept coming up with more things we could do to make more money. He started complaining that he would die of exhaustion from overwork before I ran out of steam. He was right about one thing. Our retail business was exhausting. I had learned from my childhood business ventures when to fold, so we closed up shop and I took another full-time job instead. The pay wasn't great, but at least it was steady income.

My father had always envisioned all of his children getting a college education. I thought if I got my degree, I could get a better job and that would put my family in a better position financially. I continued to work both jobs and went to school full-time at a local university. My parents and siblings took care of the children for us while we worked.

They say that trouble comes in threes. I experienced the first incident of physical abuse from my husband the day before our wedding. After the wedding our home went up in a blaze of smoke and flames. Not long after we closed down our retail business, my father passed away.

The Death of a Dreamer

My father, Tong, was a great man. He was loved, respected, and admired by his family, his relatives, his friends, and his community. I will always be grateful for the courage and fearlessness he demonstrated to me, my mother, and my siblings from the day he chose to leave Laos and wade through the Mekong River with my mother and their children. He was a diligent and industrious man, always coming up with ideas and means of taking care of his family. He worked hard his entire life, never stopping to take a break. He felt as though he couldn't rest until he secured a future for all of his children, always driving harder to give his family a better life. My mother saved almost everything he earned. Dad set aside his dreams of travel and any luxuries for himself so that he could do more for the family he loved. Up to the last day of his life, he focused on how he could help us all to experience more of the good things this world has to offer. His death devastated me — it shook us all to our very core.

My sisters and brothers were still too young to go out and find work to help support the family. My mother still didn't speak English very well and had never held a job outside of the home. It was my dad who had taken the children to school, done the grocery shopping, took care of things around the house, and a myriad of other things. He was the only one in the family who knew how to drive.

How were they going to survive? If I was a son, the responsibility for my family's well-being would have rested on my shoulders, but I was a married daughter with a family of my own. That meant that everything would fall in my mother's lap.

The sudden death of someone you love will take you down a deep, dark hole. I loved my father. I didn't realize how much I looked up to him, how much I relied on him, how much alike we both were. I didn't know how to cope without him. He had always been there, steadfast as the sun, moon, and stars in the sky. How was I going to push through the darkness that his absence left? He was the most goal oriented, determined person I knew. It was his dream that had brought us to America and put us in a house like the one he showed me on the big screen. What was life going to be like without his imagination, his sense of humor, his laughter, his wisdom, guidance, and direction? What was going to happen to my mother and my siblings?

I was the oldest and I felt responsible for my family. I couldn't let them struggle. I would not allow them to become homeless. I had to figure something out. Even if my dad was gone, that didn't mean his dream had to die with him.

After dad passed, my mom shared something with me that hit me with the force of a sledgehammer. She said, "I wish I had known he was going to go so soon. I wouldn't have let him work so hard. I would have let him buy whatever he wanted and travel the world. All the money he saved, that he worked so hard for — he couldn't take any of it with him and he can't enjoy any of it either."

This changed my way of thinking. Money isn't all there is in the world. It's a resource. It couldn't bring my father back. None of us know when our time would come. It could be a few days, months, years, even decades. The best we can do is enjoy our time here and now. Spend time with the people you love and let them know you care about them. Working hard and making money is not all there is to living.

Not long after my father's passing, my mom and siblings moved to Minnesota where my father's brother and sister lived. Being close to my dad's family was best for all concerned. My mother was suddenly thrust into the role of both parents, a role she had to master quickly with little knowledge of how. She had depended on him since she was a young girl. Now she had to learn to be independent, taking care of six children while dealing with her grief.

The little girl in me felt lost again in an unhappy marriage. I threw myself into work and school. I didn't want to think about anything else. It hurt too much. Everything had changed. My family wasn't there for comfort or to help me with my children anymore. Because I made more money, my husband and I decided that he would stay home with the children while I continued to work two jobs and go to school. I bottled up all of my emotions and focused on getting my degree. I wanted my father to be proud of me. Life outside of that pursuit did not exist for me anymore. I spent most of my time away from home, away from anything that would remind me of the pain, anger, and hurt I had compressed into tiny compartments so I wouldn't feel anything. Determined, I relied instead on the faithful comfort of hard work.

It took some time, but I finally earned my bachelor's degree – Bachelor of Science in Business Accounting. I wished my dad were alive to share that accomplishment with me, to watch me walk across the stage in my cap and gown. How proud he would have been. That's all that mattered to me. I had honored my father by fulfilling the dream of a college education for at least one of his children, even though he hadn't lived to see it.

I celebrated that special day with friends and family. We rented a sixteen passenger limousine to transport all of us to and from the ceremony. We had some wine and stopped at a restaurant for dinner and toasts afterward. I saved a seat for my father, just in case he was there in spirit.

I could not turn back the hands of time, but I could push forward. After graduation, I dried my eyes and began the slow climb out of the shadows just as my father had done many times over.

Cash, Credit, and Coping

For a while, lost without my father, I forgot about the little girl with the big vision, and the impossible dreams. I had given up on her., again. But I realized that I would need to resurrect that ferociously determined child if I were to fully finish what my father had started. I continued thinking of ideas that would help my family prosper. When I got my degree, I was able to get a better paying job, quit my second full-time job, and invest in another business venture.

I had managed to save $5,000. With it I purchased a computer and some books on reselling, wholesaling, and operating a business. I started a drop ship, wholesale/resale business. It was a lot less time consuming than trying to retail goods. I didn't need a physical store location. Instead, I found items I was interested in selling and listed them on Ebay at retail and wholesale prices, if buying in bulk. Once an item sold, I would purchase it from a wholesale vendor, and they shipped it directly to the customer. I didn't have to keep any inventory and I pocketed the profit. Eventually I made enough money in that business to quit one of my full time jobs.

Around this time, I also purchased our first home. The seller was an elderly gentleman who had been flipping houses for decades. He had a "For Sale by Owner – Open House" sign out front. We had been looking for a home for a while and decided to stop in to take a look. The seller was sitting on a rocking chair in front of the house welcoming potential buyers as they walked in.

"Did you used to live here?" I asked the man.

"No. I bought it from an old couple. The wife went to a hospice and the husband can't afford to stay here anymore so he sold it to me before it was foreclosed. It has brand new carpet and new paint. Go on. Take a look."

I smiled and thanked him for his generous response and walked inside. After a few minutes he walked in and asked if we had any questions.

"I like it. I think I want to buy it," I responded.

"This is the third one I've listed this week. The other two sold within the first two hours so put in an offer if you're serious."

"Okay. How can we make a deal today? I want to buy it and you want to sell it right? Full price. I'll take it. Do you have a PA? Where do I sign?"

"I like you," he chuckled. "Very ambitious! That's how you get things done. You remind me of myself when I started 30 years ago."

I was intrigued by the stories he would tell me of how he got into the business and what he had been able to accomplish. Later that day, I went to the bookstore and bought every book I could find about real estate investing. I bought my first house for $240,000, put in $12,000 in renovations, and sold it for $365,000. I was immediately hooked.

Ty was still a stay-at-home dad. While the children were at school, he would go fishing and hunting. My husband was a creature of habit. His drinking had been a bad habit. Fishing became his favorite pursuit, and he would go out fishing with his friends day and night – at least that's where he said he was going. I believed him until he dialed me by mistake in the middle of the night. I thought he was talking to me, but he was actually talking to another woman. I listened to the entire conversation. When I confronted him about it, he said the woman was his friend's girlfriend. But every wife has a sixth sense. When you live with someone for an extended period of time, you learn their habits. I knew my husband was being wild and loose with the truth.

I couldn't find more houses to flip. Not having a partner to help made the tasks more daunting. My drop shipment business, however, was doing great! Annual sales had reached over two million dollars. I was able to stop working full time and focus on my business pursuits alone. This gave me more time for my family. Ty still spent most of his time away from home, sometimes not returning for days at a time. I wanted my husband home with me and the kids. After all, we were a family and things were going pretty well. At the same time, it was more peaceful at home when he wasn't there. There were no intoxicated rants or hurtful insults.

I enjoyed spending time with the children. We visited Disneyland, Magic Mountain, and Six Flags. We enjoyed movie nights complete with hot buttered popcorn and plenty of candies. I shared the fantasy of the big screen with them as my father had done with me. We ate at fancy restaurants and went shopping. Lots of shopping. Truth be told, as much as I was enjoying our children's company, I was also keeping myself occupied so I wouldn't think about the pain and betrayal I was feeling. I would go anywhere, do anything, buy anything to numb the ache.

Faking it Doesn't Help You Make it

Life appeared good. I had it all. Or at least I pretended to. I had my family, whom I loved. I had more money than I had ever made in my life. I had a lifestyle that I enjoyed. But I was miserable. Despite what it looked like, I was walking around with a broken heart. My all-American dream had turned into a vicious nightmare that I didn't want to see. So I filled my life with things that would act as distractions.

At 22 years old, I paid $120,000 in cash for a Mercedes SL hardtop convertible. I fell in love with it the moment I laid eyes on it, brand-new and glistening on the dealership's lot. I just had to buy it. I debated buying a $1.9 million riverfront home but ultimately decided against it and bought an $800k home with more space instead. I wore only name brand clothes and carried $2,000 Louis Vuitton and $4,000 Prada bags. I donned a few pairs of $2,000 Jimmy Choo shoes. I wanted people to look at me and believe that I had it all together. No one would ever know about the little girl who only had one pair of shoes and picked clothing from the Goodwill store. They would see how prosperous I looked instead of how sad I was. They would envision success, and never know of the abuse and betrayal that was tearing me apart.

Shopping was my coping mechanism. I was still hurting from my father's death and I missed my mother and siblings. I was in what felt like a marriage of one. I was lonely and hungry for attention and affection. I tried to replace the love I wasn't receiving from my husband with things I could purchase at the store. Whenever my husband and I fought, he would vacate the premises, often for long periods at a time. I knew he was unfaithful, but what could I do? So I went shopping. I would go buy myself a new bag or clothes for the kids — anything to try to plug the leak in my soul.

I made a lot of money, but I didn't understand the concept of reinvesting. I just kept spending, thinking that the money would always flow as freely as it did. It would always be there to comfort me. As an idea person, in my mind, I could always manifest what I wanted. I could always make more sales and create more income There was no end to my supply of ideas and ways to make more. I had made it and there was always going to be more of the same.

When you rely on something outside of yourself for your happiness, you take the risk of damaging your delicate inner frame. I got lost in trying to live the lifestyles of the rich and famous. I drove a glamorous car, wore expensive clothes, pranced around in fancy high-heeled shoes that cost thousands of dollars. I looked and acted the part, which, by the way, isn't the mindset of the truly wealthy. I gave the appearance of confidence and power, but inside I felt broken and powerless. I was spending my life and my money instead of investing both financially and spiritually. Using money to cope with loss and grief is a recipe for disaster.

I may have looked rich, but I was digging myself deeper and deeper into a huge financial hole of debt and denial. I didn't know how I was going to get myself out. I may have been toting around Prada bags, but they didn't have any cash in them. My wallet was full of credit cards, about 15 of them, but they were all maxed out to the tune of $20,000 to $35,000 each. I charged and charged, paying only the minimum balance every month. I had incurred so much debt that no matter how much money I made, it all went to paying the bare minimum on my monthly bills. I was stressed out and depressed, but I plastered a smile on my face and kept it moving. I was up to my ears in arrears, faking it trying to make it.

But you can't fake a right mindset. You can't fake your soul's healing. You have to get those things right. Buying new things may make you feel better in the moment but there will be a price to pay for it later. Debt may be a part of the American dream but living with it can be your worst nightmare. I had done what I said I would do. I had lived up to the vision I spoke about concerning owning property and being the CEO of my own company. What I couldn't buy, what I couldn't fake was peace of mind.

CHAPTER SIX

THE HOUSE OF CARDS

American society runs on credit. Comedian Trevor Noah once shared a story in his standup routine *Good Credit, Buy Anything* about coming to America and his first attempt at leasing a car. He had the money to pay for the car he wanted, but the salesman told him there was no way he could lease the car without credit, especially since he was a foreigner. Although Noah tells the story with great humor, the fact of the matter is credit is king in America. The more you owe, the higher you go.

The bitter truth is that the more you borrow, the greater the sorrow when you can't pay it back.

The housing market crash of 2007 was the worst in the history of the United States. Nearly on par with the Great Depression, this global economic crisis was the result of a perfect storm. Most people didn't fully understand what was happening across the country and around the world. People were confused about why their mortgage rates were suddenly going through the roof. Realtors and others involved in real estate sales couldn't sell houses fast enough to keep up with skyrocketing loan rates, rates that had once been so friendly that housing prices soared, creating wealth for anyone who was in on the market. The financial bubble that sustained housing that had existed had reached its fullest capacity and burst, leaving people homeless practically overnight, corporations bankrupt, and personal lives devastated. Ours was one of the families caught in the crunch of that devastation.

When the housing market crashed, one moment we had it all, the next moment we had lost everything. Business wasn't going well and there were no houses to flip. I was spending money as quickly as I got it, believing there would always be more, but our cash flow declined steadily. Every vehicle we had, except for those I had purchased with cash, was financed. This included a $60,000

Lexus, an $80,000 GMC Denali XL, and an 18-foot boat. The bank came after every single one of these items.

It was a Tuesday evening. I had just got home from work. The kids had called me and said we were out of milk so I parked the Denali on the driveway and went inside to grab the kids so we can go grocery shopping. Fifteen minutes later the kids and I piled back outside to find out the Denali was on the back of a tow truck, slowly driving away.

"Hey, that's my car!" I yelled chasing after the tow truck.

The tow truck stopped, and the driver got out. "Are you Wendy?" he asked.

"Why are you towing my car?" I asked.

"The bank is repossessing it. If there's anything in the car that you still want, I'd recommend taking it out now," he said handing me a black 13 gallon garbage bag.

Dammit, I thought to myself. *I haven't made a payment in over three months.* I just found a job and was waiting for my paycheck to pay that off.

"I was going to pay this Friday when I get my paycheck," I pleaded. "Couldn't you at least wait till then to give me some time to pay?"

"No ma'am. I'm sorry," he said, shaking his head.

I sighed loudly and then grabbed the bag from his hand and emptied the car of our personal belongings, then watched as the tow truck drove off with the Denali on its bed. Tears streamed down my face. Everything that I'd worked so hard for was slowly disappearing in front of my eyes and there was nothing I could do about it.

The next day I drove the Lexus to work. After work, I came out to the parking lot to find the car also gone. At first, I thought it was stolen. I called the police to make a report. It turns out that it too was repossessed. They came and towed it while I was at work.

My Mercedes sports car was my pride and joy. It was the first big purchase I made for myself when I felt I had finally made it. It made me look and feel successful. I was so proud of that car — it meant so much to me. But it was only a two seater, and we had a family of six to think of. My husband

and I drove six hours away from our home to a CarMax where we sold the $120,000 car for $40,000.

We also had to sell our $800,000 house in a short sale. A short sale is an alternative to a foreclosure. It protects your credit, but it also means that you will have to leave your home immediately. Our house sold for $450,000, not enough to pay off the mortgage. We were under water like all the others who had lost their homes when the economy crashed. The cars and the boat had already been repossessed. I was in default on all of my credit cards. There were no houses to flip and even if there were, we wouldn't have been able to move them through the market fast enough to keep up with or even manage our debt. Our credit score plummeted. Because of that, we had a hard time finding a place to live. We were considered too much of a financial risk and no one wanted to rent to us. We had nowhere to go. I had nothing much to show for all the hard work I had done. Taking what little we had left, we packed up and moved to Minnesota hoping for a fresh start.

I had overstretched myself and could not meet my obligations. Our debt had become a house of cards that fell on us and everyone around us. It was a horrible and embarrassing experience which I tried to conceal by putting on a happy face. Ty didn't blame me for our financial losses, but the housing market wasn't the only thing that crashed. Our marriage up to this point had been an epic fail.

A Disastrous Marriage

Several of my friends told me that they had seen Ty with different women multiple times. I didn't like hearing it, but I didn't think they were lying either, so I confronted him. He repeatedly denied the accusations. I didn't have any proof, so what was the point in arguing about it? Although I didn't do anything at the time, I was still suspicious.

They say if you go digging for something you are sure to find it. I wanted to know the truth, so one day I decided to put a tracker in his car. The tracking system showed that Ty's car was parked at a certain location for several hours a day on a daily basis. This was a red flag for me. One night when he was out past 11:00 p.m., I called him. He was supposed to be on an overnight fishing jaunt with his buddies. When he answered the phone I asked him where he was. He told me he was at a funeral home. I checked his location, got in my car, and drove to the address. His car was sitting in front of a house that was definitely not a funeral home. There was a woman in the car with him.

I parked at a distance and walked up to his car. The closer I got, I could hear him and the woman talking and laughing. He thought I was a stranger walking up beside the car. I had on a black sweater with the hood over my head so he wouldn't recognize me as I slowly walked by.

"Do you really love me? Don't lie," the woman said.

"Of course. I would never lie to you," Ty replied.

I had to confront him, I thought. *If I leave without confronting him, he'll deny everything.* Before I realized what I was doing I had already opened the back door and jumped into the back seat.

"What the fuck!" Ty yelled looking back.

I slowly pulled the hood off my head so he could see my face. His eyes grew wide in disbelief once he realized it was me.

"What are you doing here?" I asked.

"I…I…How," he stuttered. "How…Why are you here? I ... I was just dropping her off," he lied.

"Sure. Your car has been sitting here for the past two hours. Does it take two hours to drop someone off?"

He didn't answer.

"Who are you to him?" I turned and asked the woman. "How do you know him?"

"We're just friends," she said without moving a muscle.

"Friends?" I quizzed.

She didn't reply.

"Do you know that he's married?" I asked her.

Still no response.

"She's just a friend. Stop embarrassing yourself," Ty shouted.

"I'm embarrassing myself?" I chuckled. "Or am I embarrassing you? If you want to be with her then come grab your shit and move the fuck out!"

I got out of the car, slammed the door shut and left. The woman just sat there quietly not uttering a word.

As soon as I got to my car and left, his car came raging from behind and followed me home.

He denied that the lady in the car was his girlfriend. I knew better. I went home and packed my things. I was going to take my children and go but when he returned home, he took a knife to my car threatening to deflate my tires and stab me if I dare go near it. He was not about to let me leave and told me so. I was terrified, so I stayed.

There was no longer any trust in the relationship on either side. After that last incident, Ty wouldn't let me out of his sight. I had no privacy. Everywhere I was, he was. I had stopped caring. I knew I didn't love him anymore. When he figured that out, he accused me of cheating on him. He made up his mind that I was having an affair and was trying to leave to be with another man. He again threatened to kill me if I tried.

When you don't have trust, you don't have much of anything to build on. Love and even financial security are not sufficient to keep a marriage together. The basis of any relationship is trust. Ty said he would change. He said he would do better. I really wanted to believe him, so we tried again.

After moving to Minnesota we stayed with my mom for a few months. We couldn't stay long term because our family was growing and there wasn't enough room for all of us. At this time, things took a turn for the better in my relationship with my husband. He admitted to having extramarital encounters and said that he didn't consider himself to be "good enough" for me. He felt like he had failed. He claimed that the only way he could feel like a man was by pursuing relationships with other women who needed him. Being a stay-at-home dad and not the main breadwinner was the direct opposite of everything our culture stood for. This had evidently been hard for him to get used to. He may have gotten teased by other men as well. In any case, we talked until we reached a point where we understood one other. We were both building a better life for our future and for our children. We both had a part to play and as long as we worked together, it didn't matter that the roles were reversed. We promised to do better.

A few weeks later I landed a job at a large corporation. My husband also found work. Our total income combined was a far cry from the $2 million I had been making, but since we had started from zero, it more than beat having no income at all. Though we were both working, we were still living paycheck to paycheck and still had debts to pay off. Some weeks there wasn't enough money to put gas in the car. Sometimes we had to borrow money for food. The children were growing too. I scoured clearance aisles for cheap clothes and shoes. I sold all my Louis Vuitton and Prada bags for pennies on the dollar. We took the money we made from the sale of my Mercedes and paid cash for a $30,000 house. It wasn't anything like the house we had lost but it was a place of our own to call home. We remodeled it and lived there for about a year.

Not satisfied with where we were financially, I looked for another way to increase my salary without having to get a second job. I decided to go back to school to obtain my MBA. Maybe that would open more doors into my career in accounting. I also got involved in real estate again.

My husband once again agreed to be a stay-at-home dad. We knew this wasn't the Hmong way, but we agreed that it worked best for us. I borrowed some money from my family and bought a rental unit for $30,000, fixed it up, and rented it out for $900 a month. That added $10,800 per year to our income. I used a portion of the rent to pay back what I had borrowed.

Things were going smoothly for a while, but old habits die hard. Eventually my husband found new friends and started going out drinking again, thus nullifying the promises we had made to one another. When he wasn't with the children, he spent a great deal of time fishing and hunting. He spent the weekends with his friends instead of his family. The arguments resumed as if they had never stopped. We threw things at each other, including hurtful words that neither of us could take back.

Ty had a jealous streak. He would bring friends over to the house and, after they left, accuse me of flirting with them if I was nice to them. His cousin came looking for him one day. I told him Ty wasn't home and the cousin left. When Ty got home, I let him know that his cousin had come to see him. He flew into a jealous rage and accused me of sleeping with his relative. We argued. He pushed me against a wall and struck me hard in the face, calling me a whore. He had thrown things before, threatened me before, even came close to striking me. But this was the first time he followed through. I packed my things, took my children and left him for three days. I stayed at my uncle's house and told Ty I was done. I didn't want to be married to him anymore.

When you are in an abusive relationship, there is always a honeymoon phase after an abusive occurrence. This is when your spouse or partner is apologetic, showers you with gifts such as flowers, roses, and candies, and transforms into the kind of companion you have been yearning for. It is a deceptive phase in that it doesn't last very long. It only serves to get you back and keep you in the relationship. The honeymoon phase happened several times with me and Ty. He came to my uncle's, apologized, and we got back together. Things went well between us for a little while. There was a short period of relative harmony and we had two more children. Then the cycle starts again.

Ty went out and came home drunk. The children had just finished eating and I hadn't had the opportunity to clean up after them yet. When Ty went into the kitchen, he saw a sink full of unwashed dishes, and pots and pans on the stove. Enraged, he threw all the dirty pots, pans, and dishes into the trash.

"Why are you so fuckin lazy?" he yelled from the kitchen. "Can't clean! Can't even cook me a proper meal! Why the fuck are there so many dishes in the sink?!"

"The kids just ate! I'll come clean up in a bit," I yelled from the bedroom, annoyed. I had just got home from work and had a twelve page paper due before midnight. That was a priority. I needed to get that done. But he didn't care.

He cursed and yelled at me telling me I was not a proper wife. He referred to himself as the "king of the house." He expected me to be at his beck and call, to jump or come crawling to him whenever he demanded. I yelled back telling him what I had always told myself. "I am not your slave." This brought on a torrent of rage.

Ty punched and kicked the living room wall. I stopped what I was doing to go stop him from destroying the house.

"Stop it! What the fuck is wrong is you? Why are you so mad?" I yelled at him.

"You," he said pointing his finger at me, "do you not know that I am your husband? You have no respect for me. You think you're better than me, don't you?"

"I don't know what you're talking about! You're drunk! Just go to sleep and stop yelling! You're scaring the kids!" I yelled back.

I turned around and headed back to the bedroom to finish my paper. It was almost 10:00 pm and I still had quite a lot left to do.

"Bullshit!" he shouted. "You don't have a paper due. You're just chatting online with your boyfriend. You think I don't know? I know everything that you do!" He took one of the artworks off the wall and threw it in my direction. Before I was able to turn around, it hit the wall and the glass shattered into pieces. He quickly followed me and pulled my hair, dragged me into the kitchen, and pinned me to the floor with his knees. He grabbed a knife and threatened me, letting me know that he would kill me if I ever again failed to recognize his authority or disobey him.

I thought Ty would kill me that day. He didn't of course, but he had instilled a new fear in me. I was terrified of him. I thought, *What if he is crazy enough to kill me and my entire family? How am I going to get away from him?* I got depressed to the point of contemplating suicide. I had thought about it a million times, but I couldn't do it. I couldn't leave my children alone with this man. I couldn't abandon them. My life without my dad was hard enough and I was a grown woman. How would my children handle life without their mother? No matter how I felt, I couldn't leave them like orphans with no one to love or cherish them. My children were the reason I never followed through on those dangerous thoughts of taking my own life. I knew I needed to be alive to give them the world they deserved.

My husband continued to do what he had previously done, party and drink until the wee hours of the morning. I stayed in the marriage, worked, and took care of the children and home. The children and I were always on pins and needles at home, walking around on eggshells, tiptoeing every time he was in the house. You never knew what little thing would set him off or what kind of mood he would be in from one minute to the next. It was a highly volatile environment, even more than it had been when we lived in California. If I was going to get away, I had to be careful. I had to be strategic. I had to find the courage and the means to do what I knew I needed to for myself and my children.

Parting

One night during the week Ty had his friends over drinking and singing karaoke. It was a school night for the kids, and I had to get up for work at 6:00 in the morning. He and his friends partied loudly until 4:00 a.m. I was livid. As usual, we argued. Our verbal and sometimes physical warfare had become a constant. I had considered leaving Ty a thousand times but couldn't find the courage until I saw how toxic our environment was for the children. The most dangerous time for anyone in an abusive relationship is when they decide and take steps toward leaving. I finally put together a safety plan, got a restraining order and left.

There are several reasons why women don't immediately leave an abusive relationship. Many times they have been gaslighted so much that they believe they are at fault and, if they reverted to a traditional role, things would get better. This is because society at large tends to normalize unhealthy behaviors. Machismo in men, sexuality and submissiveness in women are the hallmark of abusive relationships on a global level. The woman who ascends to the rank of CEO in corporate America is often singled out. The woman who tries to leave an abusive relationship is 70% more likely to be killed after she does (Onelove, 2017). These are sobering facts.

At the time of our separation, Ty and I owned a property together. There was one particular piece of property that was in his name only. He sold it for $40,000 cash. He tried to use it as a bargaining chip for me to return. He said he'll give me all the money if I cancel the restraining order and go back to him. I told him he can have the money. I don't want it. So he took the money and ran. Our divorce was finalized. The marriage was over. I was now officially a single mother with four kids to raise. Oddly, it was as if not very much had changed because we were used to Ty being away from home for days at a time.

The difference was that he was no longer breathing down my neck telling me how incompetent I was as a wife and mother. I no longer had to worry about where he was, what he was doing or to whom. I still had a full time job and my real estate properties. I had always maintained my independence and known my own capabilities. I knew I could do it on my own.

However, Ty's leaving permanently and our divorce was a double-edged sword. On the one hand, I felt freer and more capable after he was finally gone. On the other hand, I felt an overwhelming sadness. We had been married for 15 years. In my heart I blamed myself for our failed marriage. I kept telling myself it was my fault that he acted the way he did; something I did drove him to be that way.

Frankly speaking, I had once been in love with another man before I met Ty. There were circumstances beyond our control that prevented us from being together. I did think of this man sometimes though I never contacted him after Ty and I were married. Maybe this was the reason for Ty's constant accusations and jealousy. I now faced the reality that my children were growing up without a father and the guilt that I had broken up our home. I never wanted them to come from a broken home. I wanted them to have both parents available to them, but I had failed to achieve that for them. I could have prevented all of this from happening, right?

Wrong.

When a marriage disintegrates there is plenty of blame to go around. Blame, however, does not benefit anyone. When two people are joined together in matrimony, it takes some essential things like love, trust, compatibility, and commitment to weld it together. I didn't recognize this at the time. All I knew was the pain. I felt so much of it that I too started drinking heavily so I could feel numb.

Divorce can be a heartbreaking process. Divorcing an abuser can be even worse, whether the abuse is physical or emotional. Emotional abuse leaves invisible scars that can last a lifetime. Feelings of unworthiness, questioning your decisions, unforgiveness of yourself and your partner can all take you down a path of depression and self-destruction. I had been on that self-destructive path for a long while. My mind was cluttered with blame and accusations, mostly against myself. Guilt weighed heavily on me. Guilt for all the years I had spent working two jobs, building businesses, and going to school, leaving my husband and children alone while I focused on my goals. In all honesty, I was never around for long periods of time too. All the same, I didn't hang out getting drunk with my friends or have relationships outside of my marriage and that when I wasn't working on my goals, I was working on my family. I had to give myself credit for that.

Then again, I reminisced, maybe I worked too hard and too much. Was I as driven as my father? But surely, that was no excuse for the abuse my husband hurled at me! No, all in all his behavior was his choice. It took a while for me to realize that it was not my fault.

All the same, Ty had been my friend and confidant. When our marriage fell apart, I lost the only friend I felt I truly had. There was no one to vent to so I bottled everything up inside. I kept hoping things would get better. Although my rational half wanted it, emotionally I was crushed when the divorce took place.

Picking Up the Pieces

When I was a child we played a game where we threw a stone up into the air and had to pick up sticks before the stone fell to the ground. After my divorce, I was playing a game of pick up sticks with my life. There were all these pieces that had to be picked up and put back together, pieces of me and the life I wanted to rebuild for myself and my children.

I realized that one thing I had failed to do during my marriage was to make time for myself. When I wasn't working, I was at home taking care of my family. I had always planned trips, outings, and events for the children. I tried to include my husband in things, too. But I didn't have a social life of my own. I was still young so after the divorce, I took a little me time to cultivate a social life. I went dancing. I went out for drinks. I partied in the clubs. It wasn't an everyday or weekend thing, but it was the first time I had allowed myself to lighten up a little bit in a very long time. It was refreshing.

Later I decided I needed to spend some time with friends. I reached out to some of my old friends with whom we had lost touch over the years. Most of them were still single and living in New York City. I flew out and spent time catching up with them. It felt good to vent and talk through the divorce, my father's death, and all those pent up emotions and hurts I had been holding inside for so many years. My life up to that point had been so full of trauma and pain. Talking about it was a release.

Many times, women don't talk about their sorrows. We are told to be strong and courageous, to hold it in just like men. We carry our burdens silently. My mother never talked about the children she'd lost before coming to America. She probably never will. The pain is still too great. But I needed to talk to let the pain spill over and out so that I could be free again. Maybe my mother never felt she had anyone she could talk to. I felt grateful that I could talk things out with my girlfriends. It made me feel less crazy. Talking it out helped me to forgive myself and Ty. When you can share your pain, it validates what you went through as real. When you can face that reality, you can recover.

I didn't do any meditation or go to a professional therapist for help. Instead, I surrounded myself with people who truly loved and cared about me, my mother and my siblings — we had always been close. After the divorce we got even closer. When I was depressed and suicidal, these were the people I ran to for help. They had always been there for me when I needed them and that continues to this day. Having a close knit family has been my salvation. You can heal and move forward so much faster when you know there are people in your corner who always have your back, no matter what.

When you are dealing with situations that leave you feeling stuck, surround yourself with family and friends that love and care for you. You need people who won't blame or judge you. Don't blame yourself. There is no benefit to that either. Learn from your mistakes; forgive yourself, give yourself time to heal – then keep moving forward. Failure is how we learn. Push through one day at a time. Faith is getting up over and over again after a fall. You can see this every time you watch a toddler learn how to walk. They never give up. Neither should you.

My girlfriends and I went to Vegas a few times. I enjoyed traveling with them. We talked about goals and dreams. I realized that as a partner in a marriage, my husband and I were supposed to help each other grow. I was sorry that didn't happen but grateful for my children who are the best things I could have gotten out of the marriage. I wanted a good life and after everything was said and done, I continued to strive for that.

On my last trip to NYC, I made a vow to myself. I would never put my children in a situation where they would be homeless again. I focused on their future as my parents had focused on their own children. I was able to think more clearly. I got reacquainted with that little girl who was so determined to learn English and become a CEO. I realized that when we get lost on the path and lose our way, it doesn't mean that we will be lost forever. We have to choose. I chose to get back to work. I chose to start over again. I chose me and my children. I chose to live abundantly rather than wallow continually in my pain.

Any doctor will tell you that if you break a bone, they can set it in a cast until the bone heals, but when they remove the cast, the muscle will be weak from disuse. You will have to use the muscle, work with it to make it strong. The same goes for your heart. When your heart is broken, and it's okay to take the time to heal. But don't stay there. The pain will hurt less and less, and you will get through that dark tunnel when you choose to live. Dealing with the heartache may not seem possible at first, but all things become possible when you believe.

I was told by my community that a woman didn't need friends after she got married. Her husband should suffice as her only friend. I was taught that the only way a marital relationship could survive is if the woman gave up her friends in exchange for her husband, and that having other friendships outside of the relationship with my husband would only get in the way of the marriage. I believed and followed the tenets I had been taught but I discovered that none of those things were true. They were all limiting beliefs I had bought into, beliefs that caused me to bottle everything up inside instead of talking about it and releasing it.

I have since learned to keep good friends close by and to accept that it's okay to talk about what you are going through. Don't be ashamed of the hardships in your life. You are not alone. Others have gone through some or all of the same in varying degrees. Don't punish yourself for mistakes you made or judge yourself either. Most of us do the best we can with what we know at the time. Open yourself up to talking about your problems with someone who cares, or to a professional, if you so choose. Talking about it not only heals you and helps you overcome — it empowers others who are listening. You cannot get help; you cannot be heard until you find the courage to tell someone your story. You are important. Your story counts. You matter.

When I returned from New York, I purchased a new home for me and the kids. I was more determined than ever to find balance in my life and give my children the world. Still chasing my dream of financial freedom, I signed up for any and every opportunity that was presented to me, most of which involved multi-level marketing. I sold everything from life insurance to beauty products and skin creams. I contacted my warm market, the people I already knew who were in my circle of friends and family members, to buy my products and join my network. I met people who had made millions in these industries – but this was not for me. I tried so many things that my friends and family made fun of me and what they called my "get rich quick schemes."

I spent thousands of dollars on registrations, products, and conventions. I spent a lot of time selling, recruiting, and going to meetings. It was no different than what I had done in my own businesses. While multi-level marketing didn't work for me, I never considered it a loss. I learned a great deal from the people I met and the philosophies I was introduced to. I learned about being a team player. I learned more about business communication and marketing. I built on what I already knew. I redefined my notion of success to encompass family and spirituality along with generational wealth. I listened to great minds that I was introduced to along the way. Although I couldn't do what they were doing, everything I learned helped me in my next endeavors.

Most of all, I learned about the power of tenacity. I was encouraged to never give up. You need people around you who live that and can teach you how to do the same. I picked up the pieces of my life, accepted all that had happened, found new joy and purpose, and started all over again.

CHAPTER SEVEN

SELF-REFLECTION

"Without reflection, we go on blindly on our way, creating more unintended consequences, and failing to achieve anything useful."

Margaret Wheatley

Everything around us changes when we open ourselves up to growth and change. When you take the time to reflect on what you have learned from your experiences, you are able to move forward with a clearer vision. You observe what worked and what didn't. You take note of what went wrong and why. You discover the subconscious habits you have that may have contributed to the direction your life took. When you can step back and honestly take a look at the "woman in the mirror," you may see yourself in a new light. You can then understand how to improve your life.

Self-Discovery and Healing

In the past, every time I attempted to leave my husband, I was told by the elders in my community to return. They said I wasn't attractive, and my husband was the best I would probably ever get. They claimed I had two strikes against me: I wasn't beautiful and, if I left, I would be ostracized as a divorcee with four children. Who would want me? I not only believed this opinion, but at some point I actually believed that I wouldn't have gotten anywhere had it not been for Ty in my life. I began to accept the belief that Ty, not my hard work or my blessings, was the reason for my success. So time and again when the elders convinced me to return to the marriage, I did because I didn't feel I was good enough for anybody else.

It took time for me to process what was happening to me, to examine myself and discover what the truth was for me. What was missing? What did I want? How was I going to fulfill the dreams for my life? After leaving Ty, I had to give myself permission to dream again. And as I healed from the pain, I rediscovered myself as the person I was before all the hurt resurfaced. I began to tell myself that I am enough. I am beautiful just the way I am. I don't need anyone else to determine my self-worth. I am worthy. I am more capable than I give myself credit for. And as I opened myself up to friends and family, I began to heal and become a stronger version of myself.

In order to heal from the past perception of yourself, you have to sit down and take stock of where you are right now. How do you feel about you and why do you feel that way? "Without a clear idea of the things that matter to you or the person you hope to become … you'll continue living for other people instead of yourself" (Raypole, 2020). I had lived for my husband, my family, my children, and the elders. I had lost myself living within the parameters of what others thought I should do, feel, see, and be. I had based my entire life on the expectation of what others needed, forgetting what I needed too. I forgot that I count too.

The journey to self-discovery and healing is an interesting one with many winding turns and ups and downs. It is a journey of becoming. Like a caterpillar who turns into the beautiful butterfly displaying its radiant colors, I learned to love myself again in all my glory. I willingly shed the old me with all its trouble and despair and re-entered life with a new outlook.

When you are trying to get unstuck and move in a new direction, there are some critical questions you will have to ask yourself. The answers to these questions will help you to construct the roadmap you need for your personal journey. The following are nine steps to aid you in your journey to self-discovery and the questions you can ask yourself each step of the way (Raypole, 2020):

1. **Visualize**: When were you the happiest with your life? What were you doing then? What does happiness look like to you? What makes you feel proud of yourself? If you can visualize it, you can achieve it. Start a vision board or write things down that you would like to do. Take a few moments out each day and daydream about where you want to be in a year, two years, ten years.

2. **Explore your passions**: What excites you and brings you joy? Take cues from the things that make you smile or laugh out loud. What things give you peace of mind? What bliss would you like to follow?

3. **Experiment**: Get out of your comfort zone and do something different, something you have never done before. Take a dance class. Learn to knit. Take a college course. It doesn't have to be something monumental. Taste test a new food. It doesn't matter what it is; the goal is to try something new. This will expand your horizons. Taking safe risks can boost your self-esteem.

4. **Look at your skills**: Examine what is unique about you. What can you do well that others in your circle cannot? Do you have a skill or talent you can develop? Is there something you currently enjoy doing that you can explore and take to another level for fun or for profit? Honing skills and talents that you already possess can increase your confidence.

5. **Find your value**: What qualities are most important to you? Where do values like love, commitment, trust, honesty, compassion, loyalty, and intelligence rate on your scale? Write down those things that are important to you. What are your top three character traits? Top five? Top ten? What ranks as number one? Knowing what you value can bring focus to your life and your choices.

6. **Ask questions**: Some questions to ask yourself are: Why do I do the things I do? What drives me? What am I missing? What kind of impact do my choices have on the life I want? Be honest with your answers. Keep asking why until you get to the core of what ails you.

7. **Learn**: Be a lifelong learner. Be open to new information. Get a mentor. Download an app. Watch a YouTube video. Visit your local library or community center. Do something to improve yourself and make yourself more interesting.

8. **Journal**: Journaling is a form of therapy. It is one of the most popular ways of talking

to yourself, releasing your emotions and helping to discover what lies at the heart of your issues. "Journaling can also help you keep track of any patterns that keep coming up in your life. Learning more about unhelpful patterns can play an essential part in the self-discovery process. When you know what doesn't work, you can begin repairing it." You can also do an art journal if you're not much of a writer.

9. **Reach out**: Professional therapy can help you define goals, work through problems, identify possible career choices and/or changes. Talking to people and reaching out to other trustworthy people can help you overcome trauma. If that trauma is too overwhelming, however, don't be embarrassed to seek professional help.

The road to self-discovery and healing was a road worth taking. What I learned about myself helped me regain my confidence, self-esteem, and focus. I developed a greater desire to help other people overcome and get out of their own dark tunnels.

The Company You Keep

Although I reconnected with a lot of old friends, I soon learned that not all of them had my best interests at heart. Their intentions toward me were not all positive. But I learned from my earlier mistakes to let go of things and people that did not add value to my life. Working at the detention center while I was in high school had taught me to watch the company I keep. I tightened my circle.

You become like the people you associate with the most. Take a look at your ten closest friends. What kind of lifestyle do they have? What is their character, their basic values? Human beings imitate one another; it happens automatically. There is a proverb that bad company corrupts good morals. The people you are closest to can have a great influence on how you live your life. Did your mother ever warn you not to hang out with people whose life you don't want to emulate? Did you ever hear the saying, "If your friends jump off a bridge, are you going to follow them?" Mom was right. You are who you surround yourself with and you will develop the same traits as those you are in close contact with.

When I was young, I got discouraged by people in authority telling me what I could not do and what I could never be. Because I believed what they said, I became companions with people who didn't want much or who were also discouraged and feeling hopeless about their lives. They say that misery loves company and I've found that to be very true. Hanging around misery only brought me further down. Their crimes were my crimes. Their stories were my stories. I became guilty by association, even though I hadn't done the things they did.

There is a story of a farmer who found an eagle's egg on his farm. He took that egg into his chicken coop and put it in the nest of one of his hens who was already sitting on some fertilized eggs. The baby eagle was born a little later than the others but was brought up like the chickens, pecking the ground for food. He believed he, too, was a chicken and no one ever told him any different. Instead, he was bullied and teased by all the other little chickens who called him ugly and weird because he was different.

One day the baby eagle saw a full grown eagle flying in the sky. He was amazed. He wished he, too, could fly. He would fly away from all the misery he lived in. He was tired of pecking on the ground. He didn't like being different. He thought something was wrong with him but if he could fly like that bird in the sky he would have it made.

The large bird flew down, settled itself on the fence and spoke to the baby eagle. He asked, "What are you doing here?"

The baby eagle replied, "I'm a chicken, and all the chickens are cooped up in here."

The giant bird was confused. "What? Who told you that you were a chicken?"

The baby eagle said, "Everybody. I'm an ugly chicken. My fur is not golden yellow and fluffy like the other baby chicks. My wings are dark and feathery. I don't like pecking on the ground for scraps of food like the others do. I've eaten meat when they're not looking. They say I'm weird and different, too."

The giant bird said, "You are different because you are not a chicken. You are trying to act like a chicken, and it makes you miserable because that is not who you are."

The baby eagle was stunned. Could what the big bird said be true? Why had no one told him? "If I am not a chicken, then why am I cooped up here? If I am not a chicken, then why has no one told me so? If I am not a chicken, then what am I and what do I do?"

The baby eagle was confused and afraid. This was new information, that he didn't know how to handle. He knew something was going to change. He didn't like living in the chicken coop, eating off the ground. He didn't like being abused and called names. But it was familiar territory. He knew what to expect from one day to the next. Now things were about to change: they had to change and that was terrifying.

The big bird saw the little eagle's distress. "Don't be afraid, young one. Maybe they didn't tell you because they didn't know. Maybe they didn't tell you because they cannot fly, and if you knew, you would fly away and do what they weren't designed to. You are an eagle — the strongest, wisest bird in all creation. You were not designed to eat crumbs from the ground. You can fly and soar just like me."

The little bird was stunned. He didn't believe it. "Prove it," he said.

The big bird took the little eagle up on its back and flew high into the sky. The little eagle was elated. He had dreamed of one day touching the clouds, but he'd never thought it was really possible. He knew chickens couldn't fly. He was enjoying the ride when suddenly, the big bird purposely dropped him from such a great height it was dizzying. For what seemed like forever he spun in circles as the ground came closer and closer to him. In panic, he started flapping his long feathery wings. Then something happened. He found himself ascending as the upward draughts of wind thrust him higher. Higher and higher he flew until he reached the big bird perched atop a tall, tall tree, landing safely beside him.

The little eagle looked at the big bird. Cocking his head to the side, he asked, "How did you know?"

The big bird answered. "I saw you. I recognized you. We are alike. I am an eagle and so are you. I knew you could fly, and you can do so much more. You were born to soar."

Together they flew above the horizon.

This story has three important messages:

1. You will become like the ones you associate with the most. Write down the names of the ten people you are closest to. Take stock of their lives, their character, their values. Do they align with what you want in your life? If not, it's time to make some changes.

2. Align yourself with people who see who you are, encourage you, and bring out the best in you even when you can't see your own value. To do this, you might have to create some space between those who lift you and those who don't. Usually though, when you are working on yourself, people who mean you harm tend to fall off.

3. You don't have to keep scratching on the ground. You don't have to choose misery. Do something. Get a mentor if necessary. Follow the suggestions in this book. Take a step. Make a move. It's all up to you. Make the choice to soar no matter who tells you that you can't fly.

Some people are like crabs in a barrel, pulling each other back down when one rises to escape. In this scenario, they all lose. If you choose to continually associate with toxic, negative people, you will eventually develop the same kind of mentality. In that environment, no one is going to tell you that you can do better, and when you try, they will fight you tooth and nail to keep you from achieving.

Light illuminates darkness. It also exposes. When you begin fulfilling your dreams in the face of those who were too afraid to take the leap, it reveals that they too could have done the same and chose not to. This may make them feel anger — not with you — but with themselves. Regret is a heavy weight to carry. It can leave you bitter and leave you attacking others for what you failed to even attempt to achieve yourself.

Surround yourself with successful people. To do that, you have to identify what success looks like to you. Does it look like a healthy marriage, a sustainable career, financial freedom, or a positive mindset? Associate with like-minded people. This elevates you and them.

Put yourself in an environment of success. Remember how I told you while we lived in the refugee camp, my father took me to a movie. It was that one film that I watched over and over again as a child that had me dreaming of owning rows and rows of beautiful homes. No matter where we lived, I was always looking at new properties, always dreaming about what I could do when I had my own. I walked around million dollar estates. I was constantly looking at pictures and trying different things to get to my dream. I changed my physical and mental environment. I escaped from people who were pulling me down. I set myself up for success. Today, I finally manage a multi-million dollar real estate portfolio. It was hard work but that was definitely worth it.

When I recovered, I had to find my own way of doing things. I didn't do that alone. I had a lot of help in the process from friends and family who loved and cared about me. People who could tell me the truth. People who could support me. People who didn't judge me, and accepted me as I am. People who lifted me up. It is important that you find your tribe, your team, your circle. I learned that you don't have to do it alone. One standing alone is easily defeated. If you want to grow and upgrade yourself, lock arms with others whose character and values nourish your whole being.

Developing a Success Mindset

Writer and motivational speaker Og Mandino said, "I refuse to look back on my life and realize I had the skills, the talent, and the ability to do great things but never had the courage to try." Like Og, it was critical for me to develop a success mindset if I was going to move forward in my life.

Defining success is a subjective process. Your ideas of achievement may be different from someone else's. That does not make them invalid. You don't have to be a multimillionaire, own an island, or live at the highest echelon of society to be successful. If your goal is to be a good wife and mother with a loving family and you achieve that, you are successful. If your goal is to never be homeless, and you live in a studio apartment above a bar instead of on the street, then you are successful.

We tend to downplay what we consider small achievements as if they don't count. Are you happy? Are you fulfilled? Are you at peace? Do you have love in your life? Were you able to get through a difficult day? Have you learned how to live as fully as possible even though you have a debilitating illness? All of these things can be a measure of success. By this, we can see that the definition of success is variable, always subject to change and perception. People focus primarily on monetary success when there is so much more to it than that. I am a witness that you can be financially successful in one area, and miserable in another. I felt much more successful when I began living a life of balance than when I thought I had it all.

"Our criteria [for success] will closely relate to our social, political, economic, educational, and religious values — or ideology. And inevitably, such ideals are subjective. Moreover, since people's assessments of success are tied to their ideals, then it's the unique experience of the person being evaluated whose 'verdict' should be given the most weight" (Seltzer, 2021). What this means is that you get to define and measure what success is to you. What are you passionate about? What are your gifts? How can you make room for those things in your life? Forget what people think you should do, and do what brings you peace and joy as well as inspires you. Don't measure what makes you happy by other people's standards.

Above all, dream. Giving myself permission to dream meant I had to change my mind concerning what I believed about myself. I had to tell myself that I am beautiful, strong, powerful, creative, and caring. Developing a success mindset meant I had to master my thinking. We become and have what we focus on most. I wanted joy in my life. I wanted peace of mind. I wanted to love and be loved. I wanted my children to have a wonderful life. I wanted to live in abundance, spiritually, financially, physically, and mentally. I wanted more than my lot.

John Wooden said, "Things turn out best for the people who make the best of the way things turn out." Life for me wasn't easy. I had made some choices that caused me to go in directions I had not planned. But, just because things didn't turn out the way I expected, didn't mean I had to be stuck there. I made the best of the way things turned out by learning from my experience. I gathered the best things that came out of all of that, and used those things to my advantage. I was stronger than before. I thought more clearly. I knew what I didn't want in my life, and I learned that wanting more was okay. I allowed myself to be inspired by going through what I had been through and to inspire others.

Having a success mindset will make you unstoppable. A success mindset begins with your self-talk. I believed I was inadequate because of what significant others had told me about myself. It wasn't the truth. I had to discard that limiting belief and change my self-concept.

Research has shown that 77% of all of our thoughts are negative. According to psychologist Dr. Shad Helmstetter, most of our problems stem from our perception of a situation. We think of the worst case scenario first and the best case scenario last (Helmstetter, 1986). This does not negate the reality of other issues. It does mean, however, that sometimes it is our thoughts that get in the way.

Think about it. How many times have you created a situation in your mind that doesn't exist in reality? You thought someone was talking about you because they were laughing. You got angry or upset because of that perception but when you confronted the person, you found that you were the furthest thing from their mind. Your perception caused an emotional reaction to a problem that didn't even exist. Sometimes, because we have been programmed to see ourselves and others in a negative light, we have to scrap the whole foundation of what we've been taught, and rebuild a better one.

If you run a program on your computer and find a virus in the hard drive, it will destroy the program. That's what happened to me. I had been hard wired by a virus of negativity to believe I wasn't good enough. I operated on that system trying to please everybody and fix things to make things right. But you can't operate on a corrupted system for very long. Eventually, everything will shut down. When everything around me crashed, I realized that I would have to scrap a foundation that said I was inadequate. I had to rewire my thinking, reboot my programming to believe that I am more than enough. I knew that, in order to get up from where life had knocked me down, I had to learn to manage the way I thought about myself.

Developing a success mindset takes work and it is an ongoing process. You have to know what success looks like to you. You have to know what you want and why. When you know those two things, the how will come. You have to replace negative self-talk with a positive attitude. Our brain doesn't care whether or not what we say when we talk to ourselves is true or not. If you have allowed a virus of negativity into your system, the best thing you can do is affirm yourself. Stop saying what you are not and what you think you can't do. Speak life and love to yourself. You are worth it. Reprogram your thoughts by speaking differently about yourself morning, noon, and night — until you believe what you say.

I had been dragged down so many times by words other people said about me or to me that eventually I stopped caring. When I stopped being concerned about other people's opinion of me, I couldn't care less what they said. I challenged myself to step out and stand out. I tried new things. I took more risks. I failed forward.

Failure is not the end of the world. It is an opportunity for a new beginning. I've failed too many times to let the fear of failure stop me. Without failure, there is no growth. When you begin to look at your failures in a more positive light, it will help fuel your energy to want to do more. Failure is success turned on its head. Don't be afraid of it. Don't avoid it. Run to it. Embrace it. You can rise again.

The bottom line is this: "Despite the 'terms and conditions' you may have internalized from your environment … you alone get to decide how successful you've been. And if you feel you haven't lived up to your specified ideals, you also have the freedom (with or without professional help) to make new lifestyle choices that can transform how you see yourself" (Seltzer, 2021).

CHAPTER EIGHT

CREATING A WONDERFUL LIFE

"Don't close the book when bad things happen in your life; just turn the page and begin a new chapter."

Latoya Jackson

If you have ever flown in an airplane, you know that once you get above the clouds you can see the sun shining. It's a fascinating sight. The same happens in life. Once you get through the storm you will find that there is light beyond the dark clouds. There is a way out. There is a new path. There is a new beginning. There is another opportunity to create a wonderful life.

Overcoming Stigmas and Stereotypes

One of the key things to do is to divest yourself of negative things that have attached themselves to you. When a stigma or stereotype is attached to you, there is a negative connotation about you as a person or a group. These attitudes are used to shame people or to discriminate against them. People acting on these false perceptions of others can easily put people in danger, sometimes at the cost of the person's life. For example, people have preconceived notions about me because I am Asian. Others look at me a certain way because I'm a divorcee. Still others have a negative attitude towards me because I'm a single mom.

Women throughout history have had to deal with society's stereotypes and limitations. They have been marginalized on many levels, including access to education, healthcare, and opportunities. According to Bottaro (2021), "The consequences of this power imbalance lead to many challenges and discrepancies." These include:

- less emotional support
- increased feelings of anger and a loss of control over one's own life
- increased negative interactions within society
- higher rates of substance abuse
- increased risk of both psychological and physiological disease or illness
- higher rates of suicide

Time and time again I've had to erase stigmas placed on me by people who didn't know or understand me. True, I wasn't anything like a lot of people I knew. For one thing, I thought outside the box. My creativity was never easily reined in. I maintained that free spirit from my childhood. This irked some people and made others very suspicious of me. And because divorce was taboo, as a divorced mom with four kids, I was looked down upon by the Hmong community. They didn't know enough about me to know how successful I was, and I didn't bother to explain myself. My life was my business, and I was busy minding that, while others spread negativity and rumors.

The fact is we often fear what we do not know. Stereotypes and stigmas generated from outright lies and half-truths are often used as a way of deceiving other people into acting against someone who is different from them. It's easier to believe a baseless rumor or half-truth than to ask questions and find out for yourself. I was an unknown, a wild card. People didn't know what to make of me. In their quest to figure out my life, they made up extraordinary tales they shared with one another. In their minds I was a 'gold-digger' looking for a man to take care of me and my children.

They may have heard about my reputation as a young girl hanging out with the wrong crowd, and assumed I was uneducated and wild. They let me know in no uncertain terms that I wasn't worthy of their sons. In their minds I was tarnished goods. But no matter what they said, what they gossiped about, their negativity did not stop me from rebuilding and living my life in a way that was beneficial to me and my children.

I discovered there are three different kinds of stigma and they all applied to me (Bottaro, 2021):

1. **Self-stigma:** This is when a person believes that the negative things people say about them are true. They then begin to see themselves the same way that the stigmatizers do. The longer I stayed in my marriage, the more I was inclined to believe the stigmas people attached to me.

2. **Social stigma**: This occurs when a society makes broad negative assertions and statements about a group of people to the detriment of those people as a whole. It can happen at the level of a community, a state, or even globally. This stigma can be perpetuated through various channels including social media, the news, or local gossip. I experienced this kind of stigma from my community and on a national and state level as an Asian woman and the child of immigrant parents.

3. **Structural stigma**: This level of stigmatization is the most damaging of all. It is perpetuated in the workplace, social services, healthcare, and education.

> Because of the fear of stigma in their community or family of origin, people with mental health issues like depression and anxiety may refuse to seek help. The stigma in high school I experienced when told by the teacher that I couldn't accomplish my dream may have been the result of the teacher practicing discrimination based on my migrant status. I didn't ask for help or discuss the problem with anyone else. I just assumed she was right.

One thing I have learned is you can't change people. It's a fruitless endeavor. You will only end up frustrated and disappointed. People will make up their minds about you based on what they heard through the grapevine or what their emotional and mental state is at the time. I tried to change my husband but that wasn't my responsibility. I turned myself inside out to fit what I thought my husband needed and wanted from me. That only made me feel exhausted, depressed, and unappreciated. It was a wasted effort. You also shouldn't change who you are to fit into someone else's mold.

When I was married, I fell into the social mold of feeling I was responsible for the way things were shaping. I accepted the fact that if I did things differently and I changed, then he would change. If I just stuck in and stayed long enough, everything would work itself out over time. That may happen in some situations, but people only change because they want to or feel the need to, not because you want them to. Long lasting behavior modifications can only happen because people have the willingness, ability, and strong desire to do better. Without those foundational keys, when the mindset is destructive, when the foundation shifts, the person will return to the same behavior they are familiar with. The only person responsible for changing, learning, and growing is you. Focus on that.

One of the greatest lessons my failed marriage taught me was about love. I learned that loving myself had to be a priority in order for me to love others properly. Love and fear cannot coexist. When I was married to Ty, I was always worried about working late, having conversations with male relatives or his friends, and being engaged in any questionable behavior that would cause him to accuse me of cheating, sleeping around, or lying. A fearful life is not living at all. It is only existing, waiting for the next shoe to drop.

Fear will stop you from accessing opportunity. I passed over opportunities repeatedly for fear my husband would not approve. Courage is not the opposite of fear. Rather, it is allowing yourself to feel the fear and yet pursue the goals you want to achieve regardless of what you feel. Fear kept me in bondage: unwilling to leave Ty and unwilling to stay. I finally decided to take the leap of faith despite the fear I felt. That one move changed the trajectory of my life forever.

A Beautiful Soul

Dr. David Simon asserted, "The purpose of life is to love more and be happy" (Thorp, 2019). Do you agree with that? Finding that person you connect with down to the level of the soul, however, is easier said than done. There are three things that tend to cloud that goal (Thorp, 2019):

1. **Excess baggage**: When you carry things from old relationships that you haven't discarded, you set up roadblocks everywhere. Distrust, anxiety, trauma that you have pushed down, avoided dealing with, and ignored can flare up at any time,

especially when approached by someone seeking a relationship with you. It can show up in the form of negative behaviors including control, criticism, self-sabotage, irritation, fierce independence, ambivalence, and outright disrespect.

2. **Opacity:** To be opaque is to be unclear, shadowy, murky. When you are vague about what you want and need in a relationship, you won't know it if you see it. You have to get very clear on what you want and need to feel safe, secure, and loved.

3. **Improper vetting**: Do your research. How do you know this person? How did you meet? Where did you meet? Who are his or her friends and what are they like? How does this person handle anger? Are they actually looking for a relationship or do they want a romance? Are their values in alignment with yours? What is their relationship with their family members like, particularly their parents and siblings? Ask lots of questions. Do your due diligence.

I firmly believe the saying that people come and go in your life for a reason, a season, or a lesson. Everyone you meet is not meant to be in your life indefinitely. You will meet people who come and go to teach you something about yourself. The goal is to learn the lesson and learn it well, so you don't have to repeat it. I learned my lessons. As a result, I stepped into my genuine, unique self. As a matter of fact, I fell in love with myself. And while I was busy focusing on my future and the lovely gift of my children, I met a beautiful soul.

His name is Chang. He was an officer in the US Marine Corps at the time we met, stationed in North Carolina. After getting free from my toxic and controlling marriage, I had sworn off Asian men. I believed that most, if not all of them were like my husband, wanting a woman they could subdue. I refused to go backwards. Although I dated a little after my divorce, it was the same type of guys, men who still maintained the mindset that a woman's place is subordinate to a man, men who, like my former husband, worked a nine-to-five and spent their weekends hanging out and drinking with their buddies. I had been subject to that lifestyle once, and once was quite enough for me. No thanks!

It was Mai, a distant cousin of mine, who called and told me she had a brother-in-law that was in the military. She wanted to introduce us.

"No, thanks," I said.

"C'mon, I'm a good matchmaker," she replied. "I think you guys would make a good couple."

"No. I am done with Hmong guys."

Mai didn't give up. She asked me over and over again. She was so persistent she wore me down — I gave in and told her she could give him my number. I guessed it wouldn't hurt to talk on the phone. He lived several states away, so I didn't envision ever meeting him. Talking would be quite enough.

I went on about my life and totally forgot about my conversation with Mai. A few months later, Chang called me. The phone number was unfamiliar, so at first I wasn't going to answer the call. To this day I'm not sure why I picked it up — but I'm glad I did.

It was Chang's birthday, and he was a little drunk when he spoke. He needed a little liquid courage to reach out to me. That's why the call came out of the blue. He said hello and introduced himself. Three hours later we were still talking.

It was refreshing to talk with someone who had similar interests and goals. We discovered that we had a lot in common. He was easy going and very smart. We both had the same outlook on life. He too wanted more than just a nine-to-five. We were both looking for a life of abundance.

From the get-go, I thoroughly enjoyed talking with Chang. He was smart, kind, and honest. At the time, I was not considering a long distance relationship; but talking to him, I felt like I had known him forever. He asked if he could call the next day and I agreed. For about a month thereafter we talked every day and sometimes into the night.

When good things happen to you, you might as well know that everyone is not going to celebrate. Not everyone is going to be happy for you. You will have some haters. Get used to that.

When Chang and I first met, he had a lot of family members that were not keen on him dating a divorcee with four children. Dating a divorcee was bad enough but dating one with so many children was out of the question. After finding out that Chang and I were talking, several of his relatives tried to hook him up with other women. They constantly sent him names and phone numbers of women they thought were more suitable for a man of his caliber. When he wouldn't call them, they would send the women Chang's number and encourage them to call him.

Chang's military rank and leadership ability made him a prime candidate for a future Hmong clan leader. In the eyes of the community, dating me would harm his reputation. It was not unusual for him to get messages like: "You're not planning to marry her, are you?" "You can do so much better." and "Why do you want to be with a woman who has a million kids? What do you see in her?" I knew what was happening, but I didn't respond. I chose to ignore all the gossip and finger pointing. I figured if they could persuade Chang not to be with me, then he wasn't supposed to be in my life in the first place. I wasn't going to force the issue.

But Chang ignored them too. Their constant nagging and pushing didn't change his mind in the least. I have always admired a man who cannot be easily swayed. Even after a few of his relatives stopped speaking to him in a futile bid to get him to change his mind, he never wavered. While they were waiting for him to "come to his senses," he and I were moving forward together. When the silence didn't deter him, the gossipers said I had put a love spell on him. I know I am a powerful woman, but love spells were not my forte.

I liked that Chang was a man who didn't have a problem standing his ground. I admired him because he knew what he wanted and went for it, obstacles be damned! We agreed to meet about a month after we first talked. He couldn't leave the base and it was easier for me to travel, so he flew me out to North Carolina.

That morning of my flight I woke up to a big red pimple plopped right in the middle of my left cheek. I was supposed to be on a plane in three hours to meet Chang for the first time. There was no way I could hide that gigantic pimple behind makeup. I decided to curl my hair. If I wore it close enough to the side of my face, maybe the pimple wouldn't be as noticeable.

While on the plane, every five minutes I'd look at myself in my small wallet mirror, hoping it'd get smaller. But each time I looked at it, it seems to be getting bigger and bigger. *Why today? Why couldn't it be last week or next week? Why do I have to have this stupid, ugly pimple today?* I pouted silently to myself. *Maybe I should just get on another flight and go home. I look disgusting with his ginormous pimple. He'd probably never want to see me again after this weekend.*

"Are you going home or just visiting?" the lady sitting next to me asked as we prepared to land, interrupting my thoughts.

I tried to smile and responded, "Visiting my boyfriend but I have this nasty pimple that just popped up this morning." I pointed to the pimple and frowned. "I'm now thinking I should just get on another flight home instead of letting him see me like this."

"Oh honey. You look gorgeous! I couldn't even tell it's there until you mentioned it. You have nothing to worry about."

"Really?" I asked, looking at it again in the mirror.

"You look beautiful," she said with a reassuring smile.

After we landed, I stopped in the bathroom to once again touch up my makeup for the millionth time. *Breathe, Wendy*, I told myself. I checked my teeth again to make sure I didn't have any food or makeup stain. My fingers combed through my long black hair, twirling the curls until they rested nicely in front of my chest the way I liked. I took a deep breath and walked out into the baggage claim area where Chang was anxiously waiting for me.

I knew it was him right away as he waved and walk towards me with a smile. I smiled back. I could feel my heart in my throat as I waved back with a clammy hand. I'd never been this nervous before. Although we've talked a lot on the phone and had seen each other in video chats many times, this was entirely something else. This is the real me and we were no longer behind a screen.

He had on a tucked, white and blue striped t-shirt with a pair of faded blue jeans. He looked exactly like his pictures — tall, handsome and masculine, with a clean shaven head. He told me he worked out a lot. It was part of his job to stay fit and ready for combat at all times. I couldn't take my eyes of this handsome, sexy man. For a minute I wondered to myself, Is *this for real? Am I really here?*

"Hey beautiful," he said as his arms wrapped around my waist, pulling me up close to him, and giving me a long wet kiss.

"Hi," I replied nervously.

"You ready for our date? I hope you're hungry."

I had a real first date. Ty and I had never gone anywhere when we dated. All we ever did was sit outside my parents' house and talk. Dating after divorce was still relatively new to me. Chang showed me how it's done. We went wine tasting, did lots of sightseeing, dined at one of the best upscale restaurants, and ended the night at a comedy club where we laughed our heads off together. He offered to put me in a hotel since he lived in a one bedroom apartment so that I would be comfortable. He was, after all, still a stranger to me. He was such a gentleman at every stage. He respected my space and made sure I was comfortable. I was impressed.

One thing that will hold you back if you are going to live a life of abundance is to carry the baggage of your past into your future. You have to dump out the garbage so you don't taint your new relationships with the stench of what came before.

Being in a long distance relationship was difficult for me because I had some deep seated trust issues. After everything I had been through, I was suspicious of everyone. I expected Hmong men to be deceitful liars. Worse yet, I wanted to prove that I was right. Sometimes when you have been broken, you put everyone to the test because of what you have experienced. You have to separate the last person from the new one. Recognize that you are dealing with a different individual. If that person has the same core characteristics as the person who wronged you or did you harm, there is more work you may need to do on yourself. When you know better, and when you have done the work necessary to heal, you will choose better. You will respond differently. Of course, it's not fair to measure everyone by the same yardstick. All Hmong men aren't unfaithful or untrustworthy. All Asian men aren't abusive and controlling. I had to take the blinders off so I could see that.

A few months after our first meeting, Chang and I went to the US Virgin Islands together. While we were on our trip, someone kept texting him. I suspected it was a woman, so I asked who it was. I was right. His cousin had been working on arranging a date for him with someone else. She had provided the woman with Chang's contact information. This person reached out to him on the assumption that he was available. I responded by letting Chang know that if he was interested in someone else, we could go our separate ways after the trip.

Instead of denying what was happening, Chang shared the messages with me. He didn't lie, get upset, or accuse me. Instead, he was open and honest, assuring me that he had no intention of being with anyone else. He showed me every message and his responses to women who were clearly interested in him. He was not playing games with me; he was straightforward and transparent. I admit, I was a little taken aback by this candor.

Every night when we were apart, he would call me on his way home from work. He would call me again after he had dinner and again after a run or work out at the gym. We talked every night for hours. Despite his constant reassurances, I was still looking for faults or gaps. This relationship was everything I wanted — too good to be true, right? I had to press further to see if he was lying. If there was someone else, I wanted to know about it before I got in any deeper. I put him to one more test. I had some girlfriends call him and try to flirt with him. That failed miserably. He wasn't the least bit interested.

If you are going to be in a relationship with someone, make sure you are secure and happy with yourself first. Your insecurities, left unchecked, can drive away someone who genuinely cares about you. Thankfully, I realized that I was in a relationship with a beautiful soul, a man of quality and quiet dignity. He was patient with me. He didn't judge my past or who I had become because of it. He saw me. He recognized the times that I was speaking and acting out of pain. He loved, respected, and admired me. I grew to trust him, which helped me to gain confidence in myself again. He helped me to see the beauty in myself. With him, I began to feel beautiful again.

I stopped doubting him and I grew in love with Chang. His calm demeanor reassured me. His honesty emboldened me and made me feel safe. He saw me as capable and strong, not weak and inadequate. His love and respect for me helped heal my broken heart. He showed me that I was enough. I didn't feel like I needed to change anything about myself to be with him. He made me feel attractive, cared for, and accepted just the way I am. His love and faithfulness were genuine, and I loved him the same. I could see myself sharing a life with him. I didn't really know what love between a man and woman could be until I met him. One year later we were happily married as husband and wife.

As long as you live there will be people that will cross your path. The ones that are meant to be in your life forever will come and they will stay. They will help bring out the best version of you and of them. They will cherish and adore you. They were meant for you. Give yourself permission to dream that it's possible.

Building on a Firm Foundation

Anything you choose to build must have a firm foundation. In construction, foundations are often created with concrete. Concrete offers stability and longevity. When you are positioning yourself for success, you must also make sure you are building from sturdy material. What you build on will affect the stability of the entire structure, so make sure your foundation is strong.

The first thing a builder does is make a draft of what they want to build. You can draft your vision by writing down your long term goals and working backwards from there. You will need to do more than just writing down what you want. You have to know why you want it. Knowing your why will deepen your commitment when you don't feel like doing what you need to in order to reach your goal.

For example: I want to lose weight.

Question: Why?

Answer: To feel better about myself.

Question: Why?

Answer: Because then I will have more confidence.

Question: Why?

Answer: Because I'll be thinner.

Question: Why?

Answer: Because thin people are more popular and accepted.

Through all this circular thinking, we can see that what the person is actually looking for is acceptance. Losing weight is not the answer; neither is it the problem. The central need is, "I want to love myself more." Why? When you learn to love and accept yourself as you are, you become more confident. The result of becoming more confident may be that you lose weight because you are not using food as a substitute for something else.

You can always trace your motives when you ask yourself why. Asking why can help you figure out your goals and pinpoint the steps necessary to achieve them. How can you possibly fulfill anything when you don't have a clear vision of what you want or why you want it? Once you get to the root, you can develop the blueprint or plan. With a blueprint in place, you can figure out how to achieve what you are trying to do. You can also make changes when necessary when there is a need to take a detour.

When defining your goals, think of building from the top down. When an architect plans the construction of a skyscraper, he has to know how high he wants the building to be. What is the temperature going to be like up there? How will light, wind, rain, sun, the natural elements above and below affect the structure? When you are setting your goals, start from the top down. Determine your long term goal and then walk it backwards. What are the action steps you will need to take every year, monthly, weekly, daily? Once you have that figured out, take a few steps every day towards your goals. Buildings are built one step at a time, not all at once. Small steps are just as important as big ones.

You have to be clear about what you want. I cannot stress that enough. It's easier to push forward if you know what you are working towards. Take small steps to reach the bigger end goals. As you accomplish those small goals, you will develop the momentum needed to complete larger ones. You will soon see that your end goal is within reach.

Remember that you are not alone. You will wear yourself out if you try to do everything all by yourself. Don't be ashamed to ask for help. It takes a huge crew to build a skyscraper. Everyone involved has their area of expertise. What is yours?

Are you an amazing mother, but you hate housework? Can you hire a teenager looking for work to come and clean or do laundry for you once or twice a week? Do you love planning projects but don't enjoy being the boots on the ground? Play to your strengths; then develop a team to do the rest. Network to meet new people you can become partners with. Collaborate with other organizations doing similar things and share the financial burden and benefits. Volunteer and get to know people in your community and how you can service their needs. Make time for joy and connection.

Make sure the partnerships you develop—whether in marriage, friendship, or business—are compatible with your vision, values, and mission. There is nothing more frustrating than carrying all of the weight of a project by yourself or being overwhelmed by negativity when you are moving in a positive direction. Even when you are on your journey of self-reflection, healing, and discovery, align yourself with people who want the best for you and can see you beyond your roles, titles, and perceptions. Align yourself with people who bring balance to your life. Apply the principles of yin and yang to complement each other.

In order to change the trajectory of my life, there were many times I had to interrupt patterns, old habits that had set in. I had to switch gears and do things differently. President Theodore Roosevelt cautioned that to do nothing in a situation where you don't know what to do is the worst thing you can do. I couldn't wait for things to happen. I had to make them happen. My future didn't depend on others. I was responsible for creating the future I wanted to see. In order to do that, I had to believe that I could.

So, believe in your abilities and skills. Embrace yourself and your passion. Be open minded and step out. The only way to know if you can do anything is to actually do it. Opposition and challenges are opportunities in disguise. They help us to learn, develop resilience, strengthen our intention and desire, and form in us an indomitable will.

My new marriage began with a firm foundation. Chang allowed me to be myself and, at the same time, motivated me to be a better version of myself. I motivated him to obtain his master's degree. He encouraged me in my business ventures and later joined me in my real estate business. He was not intimidated by my intelligence or aspirations. He welcomed them. We share the same passion and work ethic. We are both driven and as such, we move each other forward. Our life is one of constant motion, a seamless ebb and flow.

Chang and I continue to work on ourselves, our marriage, our family, and our business. We purchased a few dozen houses together and grew our business exponentially, while we both worked full time jobs. To some people, corporate life and two six figure incomes were good enough. In their eyes we had made it. We didn't need to do more. But we wanted to retire by the time we were 40 years old and still be able to enjoy life, not at 65 when we were tired. There were days we would come home from an eight hour stint at our jobs and then work another four to six hours on our business. We both worked twelve to fourteen additional hours per day on the weekends. Some of our relatives said we were doing too much but our goal was always to work hard in the present so we wouldn't have to in the future.

We set a goal for both of us to be able to quit our full-time corporate jobs and work completely for ourselves. We were determined that one day we would dictate our own schedule and work only when we wanted to. In less than five years' time, I was able to retire from the corporate world, while Chang will also be retiring soon. Because we gave one another permission to dream and built the proper foundation to make things happen, we live a life that is beyond our wildest dreams. It has taken grit, passion, and perseverance to succeed. But if you never give up, it's all worth it.

CHAPTER NINE

BUILDING AN EMPIRE

Building passive income and long-term equity had been a dream of mine for decades. I thought I'd hit the jackpot when I was making two million dollars a year. I had money, a nice home, drove the finest cars, wore the most expensive clothes, and was surrounded by material possessions. But what was all that when my marriage was in shambles? My children and I were miserable. I lived in constant fear and defeat. That is not how I imagined success would be for me. I wanted more and I did the work to get it, but what I got didn't come close to the full life I truly desired.

I Shall Not Want

In 1943, Abraham Maslow developed a hierarchy of needs that has been used for decades by sociologists, psychologists, and business managers. According to Maslow, humans have specific needs that must be met in order for them to be satisfied and fulfilled. Most people only know of Maslow's hierarchy of physiological needs that include the need for food, clothing and shelter. However, they don't recognize the distinct differences between wants, needs and desires.

Many people associate want with need; however, they are quite distinct. A need is something you can't go without. You may *want* a Coke and a smile, but you *need* food and water to live. These types of needs are called deficiency needs because there are dire consequences when you don't have them.

On the other hand, when you are in want of something it means that you lack something you desire to have. Fulfilling a want is not always necessary for your existence. In fact, wants are never satisfied. They are immeasurable and unquenchable. They can change often and unexpectedly. What's more, wanting something that you do not or cannot have can make you miserable. When more is the goal in and of itself, you will never be satisfied. There is nothing wrong with wanting more. It's part of the human experience; but the real question is how much more will make you happy? What do you want more of? Why? An insatiable desire for more could negatively affect your well-being. It can leave you extremely unhappy because there is always more to have, more to buy, more to see and do.

The only thing that can satisfy want is gratefulness. It provides you with a sense of fulfillment. When you are happy with what you have, you attract more of the same. As a child, I didn't know that having Nike shoes was the in thing. I was content with the one ordinary pair. It didn't bother me that it wasn't the latest fashion. If you cannot find contentment in anything and pursue more and more things to fill a void, you'll keep wanting more, which will result in greater unhappiness. In my experience, the acquisition of things will never fill your need for love, attention, and affection; neither will it erase the pain or heartache you are experiencing.

So gratitude satisfies all that insatiable longing. Therefore, be grateful for every breath you can take unaided. Be grateful for the eyesight that allows you to see the sun. Be grateful for each movement of every limb that is working properly. Be grateful for the oxygen that gives life to your lungs and the carbon dioxide that gives life to the trees. Be grateful that you are a part of something bigger than yourself. Be grateful for every day that you wake up because it is an opportunity for you to try again.

In contrast to a heart of gratitude and contentment, there is the scarcity mentality. Because we largely live in a fear based society, our focus tends to be more on scarcity than on abundance. Most women have been trained to settle for less for fear of losing what they have. Due to cultural and societal pressure, they settle for marriages to spouses they don't really want to be with. They stay in relationships where they are unhappy and unfulfilled because of family obligations or because they don't believe anyone else would want them. They settle because they don't believe in themselves and their accomplishments. Some suffer from an imposter syndrome, believing they are not good enough to excel, even where they are equipped and trained to perform at high levels. Their basic needs may be met, but at the apex of Maslow's scale is the need for self-actualization. Self-actualization is the desire to become who you really are at your core, to be your best self. For a great many women that is a gaping need.

A scarcity mentality causes you to believe that you will run out of the thing that you need, want, or desire. It is the belief that there will not be enough or that someone else will get what's yours, or that you are not qualified or worthy to receive what you truly desire. Scarcity says that you will never be able to catch up with your bills, that you will never have enough money to invest, that opportunities are limited to you. Scarcity tells you that you are not pretty enough, smart enough, thin enough, good enough, not the right gender, color, culture, or race to receive what you desire.

A prosperity mindset, on the other hand, believes that there is plenty of everything you need in the universe. There is plenty of love. There is more than enough money to go around. There are tons of new ideas. There is an unlimited supply of peace. There are more eligible partners for you to choose from. There are no limitations. A prosperity mindset says that everything you want, everything you need, everything you desire is available to you when you learn how to access and attract it.

If you are ever going to get beyond living to only meet your basic needs, it is crucial you understand what you are asking for — whether it is a want or a need — and why you desire to have that thing. It is important that you understand the differences between the three.

You have to get to a place where you can say with confidence, "I shall not want." Maybe you think you are qualified for only the position you find yourself in right now, no more. Maybe you think that is all you are capable of. Maybe you're afraid to demand more because of a fear of failure. I highly recommend you step outside that limitation. What is it that you truly desire? Are you afraid of being criticized or rejected? Do you think that what you have is the best that you can get? Whatever you desire is waiting for you when you overcome your fear.

Finding Financial Freedom

Financial freedom has always been a dream of mine, even when I didn't exactly understand the concept. What that means to me now is that I don't have to work so hard. I can work smart and make more than enough money to support my family. It means not working two jobs, not clocking into a nine-to-five every day of the week. It means being my own boss, deciding when, where, and how I want to work. It means building my dream, not spending my life building someone else's. Financial freedom is about making the money I need to walk away from things that don't serve me.

You have the freedom to choose. Own that power. When looking for a partner, don't settle for someone you don't think you'll be happy with in the long run. You are worthy of the loving, caring relationship you desire. If you want a better paying job, go to school, get some training, find a mentor, ask for what you need and learn from others' experience. You don't have to be ashamed or afraid of wanting more. Set goals and do something about it. Don't just sit around wishing and waiting. Make a plan. Develop some intensity. Add some fuel to the fire of your dreams.

Motivational speaker Jim Rohn once said, "Discipline weighs ounces and regret weighs tons." Discipline yourself to position yourself for success in whatever area you feel works for you. Write down those long and short term goals. Partner with someone who will help you reach them. Your partner doesn't have to be a spouse. It could be a family member, a friend, a teacher, your boss, or someone you met at the grocery store who has similar interests and goals. I believe in fate. If you are pursuing your dream, you will inevitably meet people along the way who will help you. But you have to make a move. You can't drive a parked car until you turn on the engine and put it in gear. Discipline yourself to put in the work so that you don't want for anything.

Chang and I have chosen real estate as our path to financial independence. We purchased our first property together as a live-in flip. This meant we lived in the house while remodeling it. The entire house was painted; the floors in the dining room, kitchen, and bathroom were retiled; new kitchen cabinets with stone countertops and tile backsplashes were installed; and all the appliances were replaced. We had lived there for about a year before deciding to flip it. It took us three months to completely remodel the whole house. Living in a construction zone was hard, but we made it work. The benefit of a live-in flip was that we lived there, so there was no rush on remodeling, and we could work on the house whenever we wanted, day or night. We sold it a few months later and walked away with $56,000 in profit.

A live-in flip comes with both advantages and disadvantages. Living in an area that is undergoing construction can be immensely frustrating and chaotic if you are not accustomed to it. Debris has to be contained, so there might be plastic sheets hanging everywhere and tools and materials scattered about as the work is being done. If you're doing a kitchen remodel with a stone countertop, you might have to live without a functioning kitchen for weeks while waiting for the kitchen to be measured and the stones to be cut and installed.

Occasionally, though, the positives outweigh the drawbacks. If you're new to real estate investing, a live-in flip is a wonderful way to get your feet wet and familiarize yourself with the process without taking a large risk on an investment property. Additionally, the interest rates on a mortgage for a primary residence will be far lower than those on a mortgage for an investment property, resulting in a reduced monthly mortgage payment. It also doesn't need a 15–20% down payment, which is needed when buying a rental property. Depending on the financing program, the minimum down payment for an owner-occupied property could be as little as 0% to 5%. The live-in flip method is likely one of the best starting points for those with limited funds who wish to begin investing.

If you do not have enough cash on hand, which most people don't, to pay in full for the house you want, you will need a mortgage loan. In terms of financing, there's a wide range of possibilities. The type of loan for which you qualify will largely be determined by your goals, your income, your credit, and the amount of money you have saved up for a down payment. There are numerous state, city, and county programs that will provide down payment and closing cost assistance. It is feasible to purchase a home without having to come up with any money from your own savings. To find these programs, you just have to search for them.

Here are the two types of loans that we've used and are the most common:

- Conventional loans: This is the most common type of mortgage loan, representing over 75% of all home loans in the U.S. These loans are NOT backed by the government and come in two packages: conforming and non-conforming. Conforming means it "conforms" to the set of standards put in place by the Federal Housing Finance Agency (FHFA). Non-conforming means it does not meet the FHFA standards. Conventional loans require a minimum FICO score of 620 or higher and a higher down payment than some government loans.

- Government-insured loans: These aren't actually loans provided by the U.S. government. The U.S. government isn't a mortgage lender, but it insures loans to help Americans become homeowners. There are three types of government-insured loans: FHA, USDA, and VA. FHA loans are backed by the Federal Housing Administration. They require a minimum FICO of 580 with 3.5% down. USDA loans are backed by the U.S. Department of Agriculture and do not require a down payment, but you must purchase in an eligible area and meet certain income limits to qualify. VA loans are backed by the U.S. Department of Veterans Affairs. They do not require a down payment or a minimum credit score but are only provided to members of the U.S. military (active duty and veterans).

We have acquired many of our properties with the assistance of these loans. The procedure was the same for the second house, as well as the additional homes that we jointly purchased. We tore down walls, installed additional bedrooms and bathrooms, finished basements, constructed new decks, and installed brand new flooring, kitchen cabinets, and stone countertops. Larger projects and any tasks that require permits such as removing structural walls and plumbing and electrical work, were carried out by licensed and trained specialists.

I was pregnant during our second remodel, which made things a little more challenging. Chang was responsible for a large chunk of the job himself because I couldn't contribute very much. After the renovations were finished, instead of selling the house, we concluded that renting would be a better option. The mortgage was $1,400 and the rent was $2,495. This resulted in a passive income of $1,095 per month for us in the form of net rent.

For the following houses, live-in flips were no longer a viable option, especially with a small child in the house. We had to change our strategy to focus solely on the BRRRR methods when purchasing future investment properties. We went on to acquire several more single-family and multi-family dwellings using the BRRRR method. We still did a lot of the remodeling ourselves, but we hired contractors to help with the major tasks so that we would have more time to spend with our families. By using the BRRRR method and by hiring help, we were able to completely remodel each house in a matter of weeks as opposed to months.

So, what is the BRRRR way of investing? It's a strategy that numerous investors adopt to generate passive income. Imagine owning ten properties, each of which generates $1,095 in passive income each month. This amounts to $10,950 each month! That is sufficient to take the place of one or two full-time jobs! Each of our long-term rental properties brings in between $800 and $1,200 a month in profit.

So, what does BRRRR stand for?

- **Buy**
  The first letter in the BRRRR method stands for "buy." Although every step in the procedure is crucial, this is one of the most crucial. Research is necessary during this period to ensure that the property you are purchasing will be a wise investment. It's easy to get pulled down if the math doesn't add up. The home you are purchasing must perform effectively as a rental and have enough equity.

- **Rehab**
  The second letter stands for rehab. An extensive cost-benefit analysis must be performed throughout this period. An updated home will yield higher rent, but you must also be careful not to make excessive upgrades that will cost more than what you can recoup through rental income. Another crucial factor to take into account is how

much money you will have available to complete the project. You don't want to run out of money in the middle of a project.

- **Rent**
  Once the rehab is completed, then you'll have to locate a tenant and execute a lease. A copy of the lease is needed for the next step. To lower the chance of unsatisfactory tenants, vacancies, and evictions, exercise due care when looking for the ideal tenant. You can lower your risk by checking potential tenants' credit and background. Most landlords demand that tenants earn at least three times as much as the monthly rent. Anything and everything can go wrong, so you should take steps to reduce your risk as much as possible.

- **Refinance**
  Once rehab is completed and you have a lease in place, it's time to find a lender to do a cash-out refinance. The majority of banks demand a six-month

holding period after a purchase before approving a cash-out refinance. Due diligence is important because every lender is unique. Some may charge higher fees than others, and not all may satisfy your financial requirements.

- **Repeat**
  Finally, after refinancing, you can utilize the money to purchase another house and re-start the process.

BRRRR Example:

Purchase Price	265,000
20% Down	(39,750)
Mortgage Loan (Conventional Loan)	225,250
Rehab Cost (Out of Pocket)	(20,000)
After Repair Value (ARV)	385,000
Refinance - Cash out at 75%	**63,500**
Monthly Rent	2,695
New Monthly Mortgage	(1,600)
Monthly Net Rent Income (Passive)	**1,095**
Annual Net Rent Income (Passive)	**13,140**

Here is an example of one of our BRRRR properties. We paid a total of $265,000 to acquire the property and put in $20,000 in renovation. Based on the improvements we made, the property was valued at $385,000 after remodeling. We rented it out for $2,695 per month, and then six months later, we did a cash-out refinance and were able to get a check for $63,500, which is a little more than the total amount we put into the house. We then used that money to purchase and renovate another property. The new mortgage payment was $1,600, which then yielded us $1,095 per month in passive income. We will continue to earn that passive income, $13,140/year, for as long as we own and maintain the property. Repeat this process ten times with ten properties and that's a total of $131,400/year. Times it by one hundred properties and that's $1,314,000/year! All passive income! This is how we achieve financial freedom.

On your first BRRRR property, there may be some growing pains, missteps, and challenges, but it's all experience. As you move from one property to the next, you will become more informed and knowledgeable. It takes time to accumulate all the properties and achieve financial freedom. It is difficult and will require patience, effort, and attention. Learning the profession and determining what works and what doesn't may take many years. Even if not all investments pan out as expected, never give up and keep trying!

Working Hard Versus Working Smart

The butterfly gains its wings in stages; they do not develop overnight. That fuzzy caterpillar you see crawling around isn't just eating every leaf in sight: it is developing and growing. It is storing the energy needed to become all that it is destined to be. There are very few things in nature or in life that are developed quickly. Your development will take time as well. I know sometimes it's difficult and discouraging but that doesn't mean it's not possible. It takes both working hard and working smart.

I spent most of my life working hard. That's what I learned from my parents. All the same, I saw how devastated my mother was at the loss of my father because she had depended on him to take care of most things. Since I had always wanted to be more than a housewife and mother, I felt I had to do more. It was several years, particularly, during the writing of this book, before I realized how much like my father I actually was. I demanded so much of myself and worked hard, though I wasn't necessarily working smart. I wasn't using my time and money well. Even though I spent a lot of time away from my family hoping to gain financial freedom for all of us, it didn't pay off as expected.

Of course, hard work is essential if you are going to succeed at anything. If you are working at a job you can be sure you won't stay long if you don't have a good work ethic. No one wants a lazy employee. If you own a business, you must know that your clients will want someone who will go the extra mile for them. You don't get paid the big bucks for sitting around the water cooler all day. Similarly, if you want a new love in your life, then you have to work hard at loving yourself before you can give love. You cannot give birth to anything in this world without labor.

At the same time, hard work doesn't have to be tedious and grueling, especially if you are engaged in doing what you love. If you want to achieve anything, it will require putting in time and dedication. Some things may happen quickly. Most things don't. Healthy marriages don't start at the wedding. They were growing from the moment you knew that you had met the one. The wedding only serves as the announcement to the world that you will be taking the journey together. Similarly, a business may take decades to grow to the level you desire.

I've come a long way and learn to work smarter by leveraging my time and developing residual income. You can learn to work smarter in any area of your life. Figuring out how to work smarter is based upon what you are trying to do. Do you want more time for yourself and your family? Do you want to make more money without having to get another job? Is a work/life balance your goal or do you want to get more done in the course of a day? Maybe you have decided that you have worked hard and long enough, and your present goal is to aim for a better quality of life. Knowing the reason why you are working so hard will help you plan out how to work smarter.

When Chang and I worked together on our rental properties, we learned to be efficient with our time. We noticed that a lot of landlords were driving out to their properties to collect their rent money. It was a tedious process. The tenants had to be given 24 hour notice before the landlord could visit the property, and the tenants might not be available at the time the landlord was visiting.

Property managers could go out to the house only to find that the tenant was avoiding them or is confrontational. When the landlord did get the money, he would then have to take it to the bank to deposit it. Chasing people around for a rent check could be a daunting task for all involved.

Chang and I didn't want to set up our business like that. We own quite a few rental properties, and that kind of system would have entailed way too much time running around and chasing our tails. Instead, we invested in an online system. All tenants get an automated notification when their rent is due. They are all set up to pay online. Any late or miscellaneous fees are also calculated by the online system and added to the amount due. When the rent is paid, the tenant can print a receipt from the system and the funds are deposited directly into our business account. The only thing we have to do is check on the sixth of each month to make sure all accounts have been paid and verify the accuracy of deposits. Investing in an online system may have cost us a little more time and money up front but the investment paid off quickly in hours and dollars. Spending those dollars to get the system set up and installed made absolute sense.

There is very little that can be achieved without hard work but while you are working hard, remember to also be very strategic about what you are doing. Don't burn yourself out trying to do it all. Working smart means finding efficient ways to do at least some things better. Working smart and working hard go hand-in-hand to give you a life far beyond what you ever thought was possible.

The Streams in the Valley

No matter who you are, how much money you make, or how you live your life, you will have both mountaintop and valley experiences. Mountaintop experiences are those times when you feel that you are living at the height of possibility. You are achieving your goals and dreams. Your vision has proven itself. Life is good. Valley experiences are those where you feel low. You may feel hopeless and tired, discouraged and depressed. You may be facing some critical choices, decisions, or a catastrophic occurrence. The COVID-19 pandemic of 2019 brought the entire world down to the valley at the same time.

They say that experience is the best teacher, whether it's yours or someone else's. Because my first husband and I lost everything in the 2007 housing crash, I knew I would have to do things differently regarding my real estate business if I was going to protect myself. I had to make sure Chang and I would not be dragged down if anything similar happened. I had promised myself and my children that we would never be homeless again and I was determined to keep that promise. Being of like minds, my husband and I positioned ourselves with multiple exit strategies and multiple streams of income from the beginning. We expected the best from our ventures, but we also prepared for the worst case scenario.

In 2019, no matter which side of the political divide you were on or where you lived, COVID-19 reared its ugly head in your city or town.

Chang and I also owned several properties including several vacation homes in Florida, another state highly impacted by COVID-19. Our vacation homes were located in high demand, gated communities with nearby waterparks. These homes all featured amenities similar to those of upscale hotels, including fully stocked kitchens, private pools and spas, game rooms, and some even with private theaters. There were four-, five-, and six-bedroom homes of between 2,000 and 4,000 square feet of space. Guests rented short-term or long-term depending on their need. Renters included people looking to visit the beaches, Disney World, or Universal Orlando.

Vacation rentals were prohibited in Florida during the national lockdown. All of our beautiful vacation rentals sat vacant for a month or more. Due to this, many vacation homeowners who had mortgages were in danger of going into default. For several of them, it served as their primary source of income. They relied on the money from those vacation rentals to pay their mortgages. Even if no money was coming in to pay the bills, they still had to be paid. The federal government announced a moratorium in an effort to assist with this, which gave borrowers the choice to forego payments, reducing mortgage defaults and foreclosures. While many homeowners gave up and placed their homes up for sale, some were even willing to take a loss, others jumped on the forbearance plan. However, Chang and I were prepared for the pandemic, and when the revenue from our vacation rentals stopped, it didn't have a significant impact on our finances. We were less severely impacted financially when businesses started closing their doors because we had planned for the best and the worst.

Everyone goes through a valley experience. We hit rock bottom. We slide away from where we really want to be. Something in our lives hits us like a tsunami and we lose control of everything we thought we had a grip on. Yet, streams can also be found in the valley, a continuous flow of supply from places, people, and events you didn't expect. Position yourself to receive even in times of drought. Be open. Be understanding. Be compassionate. Put things in place like life insurance and a will for you and your significant other. If you own a business, work smart and hard. Don't spend everything you earn. Save and invest some. If you are unhealthy, now is the time to take better care of yourself. Get rid of excess baggage emotionally, physically, psychologically, and spiritually so you will be better equipped to handle anything that comes your way.

One of the many lessons I've learned since the 2007 crash, when all of my cars were repossessed, was never to depend solely on my 9–5 salary to finance a car. When I lost my job, I lost my income and, therefore, was unable to make the required monthly payments. As a result, I lost everything.

Since then, I've discovered a way to use real estate as leverage to pay for those material possessions so that if something similar were to happen in the future, I wouldn't be as severely affected by it.

Here is an illustration of a situation I went through with a relative and he was given two options to choose from.

Breakdown – Option 1	
Car price	36,000
Down payment	(10,000)
Total loan amount	26,000
Total interest paid at 6.9% (over life of loan)	5,907
Total loan & interest paid	31,907
Monthly payment	443

Breakdown – Option 2	
Car price	36,000
Down payment	(2,000)
Total loan amount	34,000
Total interest paid at 6.9% (over life of loan)	7,619
Total loan & interest paid	41,619
Monthly payment	578

He desired a $36,000 vehicle. He had a down payment of $10,000. Which of the following two possibilities, if given, would you pick? Options 1 or 2? Due to the smaller payment and potential "savings" of $9,712 in interest over the course of the loan, most consumers will pick option one.

I advised him to select option 2, and I'll explain why. He would have to pay a total of $41,907 out of his own pocket if he chose option one. He would possess a asset that, after six years, would no longer be worth the value he paid. Therefore, the plan is to use the $10,000 down payment to buy a real estate asset that will appreciate in value over time rather than a car that loses value.

The plan was to rent out his current property while purchasing a new home to move into. Instead of the $10,000 he would have put down on the car, he would use $7,500 of it to put down on a $250,000 house. He would only need to put down 3% for the home loan. His mortgage payment would increase from $1,100 to $1,500 as the new house is a little more expensive, but it also has more square footage. He would then rent out his old house for $1,895, which would give him a net rent income of $795. This would cover the $400 difference between his new mortgage and his old mortgage, keeping his mortgage payment the same. It will also cover most of the car payment, bringing his total out-of-pocket portion to only $183.

Why choose option two?

Purchase price of new house	250,000
3% down payment	(7,500)
New mortgage payment	1,500
Current mortgage payment	1,100
Difference	(400)
Rent from current home	1,895
Net rent income (less mortgage of $1,100)	795
Difference in mortgage payment	(400)
Car payment	(578)
Total payment out of pocket	(183)

His entire out-of-pocket cost for the car would only be $15,176, which includes the $2,000 down payment and $183 per month over the course of six years. Additionally, the $795 in net rental income would cover the majority of his new mortgage payment once the vehicle is paid off in six years, lowering it down to only $705 per month.

Now, isn't that better than paying the mortgage of $1,100 per month plus $41,907 over the course of six years? This is the knowledge I've learned from my valley experience.

What you can gain from your valley experiences is knowledge. You will learn about yourself and how well you handle crises. You will learn to either be strong or fold. You will learn interdependence. You will learn more about your hidden weaknesses while your strengths come to the fore. You will learn more about your brilliance and how much more amazing you are than you ever knew, that is, if you don't allow the valley experience to break you.

The bamboo tree grows underground for about ten years before it sprouts. But once it breaks through the ground, it can withstand some of the fiercest weather conditions possible by bending without breaking. Because of its ability to bend, it can stand up after the storm is over. Oak trees are one of the strongest trees on earth, yet they began as a small acorn. It doesn't matter where you begin or what your circumstances become; you too have the ability to weather any storm. You may have to bend sometimes to withstand the winds and torrential rains that come through your life. You may be hidden underground for longer than you would like. Your gifts may seem to have gone unnoticed. Your greatness may not yet be revealed to the world. But don't get discouraged. There are streams in the desert. Be patient. Be prepared. If you never give up, your time will come.

The Success Cocktail

"No matter where you are in life or how bleak things may seem, the goodness as well as the strife brought you to this point. Moving into abundance means counting your blessings — even the events, people or afflictions that don't look like blessings. When you can vibrate on that level of all-inclusive gratitude, you're plugged into a greater frequency of spirit and potential and your ability to receive more takes off" (Desai, 2014).

There is a definite recipe for success. The ingredients include hard work, a clear vision and strategy, positive affirmations and associations, patience, confidence, and determination.

As I mentioned earlier, all my life I dreamed of having financial freedom though I didn't always understand what that meant. I thought it meant having beautiful, expensive, material things. But there is much more to financial freedom than possessing things. Freedom is not free. It will always cost you something. In order to gain financial freedom, you will have to give up time but if you invest that time in perfecting your desire, you will watch your dream unfold. If you invest your time wisely, you will see your investment of time multiplied back to you. Success involves investing your time and attention in things that not only add, but multiply.

It doesn't matter where you start. Just start. You might say that you don't have anything to start with. That's not true. If you have an idea of what you desire and why, start there. Create your roadmap and start on your journey. The longest mile begins with the first step. If you never move, you will never know how far you can go. I had to start from scratch multiple times. There were times when I had no idea what I was doing or if I would ever achieve my goals but that didn't stop me from moving forward. Now my husband and I have a monthly passive income of $60,000 per month and owned a multi-million dollar real estate company that generates multiple streams of income —

passive and active. Now we have financial freedom.

Be the change you want to see in your own life; then you can begin changing the world. Don't give up until you win, and when you fail, start again.

If I were to give you a recipe for success, the ingredients would be as follows:

- Mix 99% sweat equity in combination with a positive mindset. Without these two ingredients in the right proportions, your mission will be impossible.

- Add a large dose of vision with strategy. You need to know what you are aiming at. Without a vision, you will exist in life but you will not live abundantly. Set clear, attainable goals with dates attached; then strategize how you're going to reach them.

- Develop a team who will assist you in creating your product. You will need their assistance whether the product you are creating is a healthy family, a renewed mind, a nutritional goal, or anything else. Surround yourself with like-minded positive people who are driving in the same direction as you. If you are moving and you get stalled out, it helps to have partners to push.

- Stay positive. Watch what you say when you talk to yourself. Use positive affirmations. Complete a vision board or notebook with pictures of the things you desire.

- Be patient. Take a lesson from the praying mantis. Learn to wait. Waiting doesn't mean standing still. Work, prepare while you wait for the opportunity to come. Don't rush anything. Avoid making hasty decisions out of fear and false beliefs. Remember that there is abundance in the universe.

- Build your confidence by taking on new opportunities. Learn from your experiences on the job, at home, and from other people through networking. Introduce yourself to one new person a week. Widen your circle. If you're shy, just say hello or give someone a genuine smile and see what happens.

- Stay true to yourself. Follow your instincts. Listen to those gut feelings. Embrace, love, and respect yourself. You have a lot to offer. You are an incredible, phenomenal person.

- There's an old saying, "Love isn't always passion, and passion isn't always love." But when you are passionate about what you're doing, your work becomes your calling and the thing that drives you to perform at high levels. Outcomes are easier to achieve when you love and believe in yourself and what you're doing. Do what you love with a red-hot fervor, and what you need will come to you in due time.

CHAPTER TEN

THE CONCLUSION, BUT NOT THE END

My definition of success changed at various stages of my life. At one point in time success for me meant getting a job with a big paycheck. I thought when that happened I would have it all. When I finally got that big job as an Accounting Manager and then a promotion to Controller, I had achieved my goal of getting a big paycheck. I had the title and the pay, but I didn't have a lot of free time to go anywhere or do anything. I was working tirelessly for someone else. I was trading my time for money.

If I stopped working, the paychecks would stop coming in.

Then I thought success would be working for myself. My dream was always to become a CEO of my own company, but I didn't really think about how I would get there or what kind of company I would have. I knew I could easily start a company and make myself CEO but having the title didn't mean I was successful. I started several different business ventures trying to find my niche. I learned what worked for me and what didn't. I met people who encouraged me and instilled in me new insight and wisdom. I even made millions of dollars. Looking in from the outside, it appeared that I had everything — a family, a big house, nice cars, a boat, and fancy clothes. People really thought I had it all. I may have looked successful, but I wasn't. I was drowning. I was not happy. I was stressed to the max.

Losing it all put me in a position to do some self-reflection. I realized that success for me was much more than making lots of money. Success had to include joy and peace. To be successful meant I also had to be happy. I had to change my mindset. I had to learn to think differently, to be more positive. I had to learn to trust again, to love again, and to accept being loved the way I am. The end goal was still financial freedom, but that freedom included love, joy, and peace of mind.

I never imagined I would put all of my adventures, missteps, and mistakes down in a book. There were times when I couldn't talk about any of the things that I endured without bawling my eyes out. You know you're healed when you can talk about it without tears, shame, or regret. I learned. I grew. I am healed and I have overcome some of life's greatest challenges because I accepted and benefited from life's lessons.

Today, I am happy just being home with my children. We have six – three boys and three girls. I enjoy spending time with my family. I have no desire to drink, go shopping, or buy expensive things to distract me from my emptiness anymore. I have found joy and peace.

My two oldest are off on their own now. My oldest daughter has a bachelor's degree and her own little family. My oldest son owns his own home - his first piece of real estate and one of many to come. It was tough for my children to go through all the traumas in our lives: witnessing abuse, the subsequent divorce from their father, and the move from a place of opulence to barely getting by. Children often can't understand the reason parents do what they do. They may not comprehend everything you've done to keep them safe or why you work so hard to give them the best possible life. They may not even discern your efforts to make sure they're taken care of and never have to struggle as you did. You can't let yourself get weighed down by this. You have to give them time to heal, recover, and mature. Just as you have learned through life's lessons, they too will understand theirs in their own time.

The Best is Yet to Come

Langston Hughes wrote, "Hold fast to dreams, for if dreams die, life is like a broken winged bird that cannot fly" (Langston Hughes, 1967/1992).

If you have a dream, never let it go. Hold onto it for dear life. The quality of success in your life depends on that and the action steps to take to achieve it. Refuse to live your life like a broken winged bird unable to fly or reach your goals. Give yourself permission. Permission to dream. Permission to grow. Permission to be the best you can be. Don't let anyone tell you otherwise. Slay all the dream killers and naysayers. Find a mentor. Get a coach. Get wisdom and understanding. Find an equal partner to work with you. It doesn't have to be a spouse. Create multiple income streams. You need at least seven to be independently wealthy.

Develop GRIT:

- Gratefulness,
- Resilience
- Intensity
- Tenacity

Pursue your passion and persevere. Work from a growth mindset and remember that failure is an opportunity to grow to the height of your abilities. Banish fear by stepping out and doing what others say you can't do. None of your goals and dreams is impossible unless you believe they are. You have to make an attempt. There will be ups and downs, highs and lows. This is the normal course of life. But nothing beats failure more than the courage to go for it again and again.

Chang and I continue to build our real estate portfolio. Our financial goal is to reach $200,000 per month in passive income over the next five years. We work together as a team in our business and our relationship. Our goal is to be able to leave more than enough for our family so that they will be well taken care of in this life far beyond ours. Spiritually, I continue to grow and be open to learning more about my purpose in life. I am learning to let go of control and allow myself the joy of discovery.

Don't forget to add a generous portion of gratitude to your success cocktail. You will need it in order to move into a place of increasing abundance in your life on every level. Everything, even the events and circumstances that pained you, can help propel you to a greater destiny. Follow the recommendation to, "Take actions that move you onto a productive path so you can be in harmony and alignment with your limitless potential and your authentic soul signature" (Desai, 2014). Be very specific about what you want, need, and desire. What are your financial goals? What are your relationship goals? What's your dream for yourself, for your family? Are you still asleep or have you awakened to the possibility of a life beyond your wildest dreams? Give yourself permission to dream big and never give up because the best is yet to come.

FOR YOUR INFORMATION

Following are a few ideas and additional information to help you along your transformative journey:

- If you are being abused and need help, advice, or safety tips, contact the National Domestic Abuse Hotline at 1-866-331-9474, or text 22522. For more information on domestic abuse and how you can help someone you know and love, visit thehotline.org. All calls are anonymous.

- If you are Hmong and would like help concerning domestic abuse, call the Hmong American Women's Association's 24 hour WI Hmong Family Strengthening Helpline at 1-877-740-4292, or 414-930-9352 during office hours.

Hmong Specific Resources:

- Hmong American Women's Association Inc. (located in Milwaukee, WI): https://www.hawamke.org/

- 24/7 Hmong Helpline for the state of WI: https://www.bbwpcoalition.org/helpline

- Freedom Inc (located in Madison, WI): https://www.freedom-inc.org/

- Cia Siab Inc (located in Lacrosse, WI): https://www.ciasiabinc.org/

- Transforming Generations (located in St. Paul): https://www.transforminggenerations.org

These organizations currently have Hmong advocates:

- Harbor House (located in Appleton, WI): https://www.harborhousewi.org/

- Safe Harbor (located in Sheboygan, WI): https://www.sheboygansafeharbor.org/

- To learn more about Hmong history and the Hmong people's contribution to the Vietnam War, check out the references at the end of this book.

- Or if you're in Minnesota, check out the Hmong Cultural Center Museum in St. Paul, MN.

Are you interested in starting your own business or developing a non-profit organization?

- Check out your local Small Business Administration (SBA) and Service Corps of Retired Executives (SCORE) for free or low-cost classes and assistance with developing your business plan, accessing grants, small business loans, mentors, and more.

Are you interested in getting a college education?

- Start at your local community college. Classes are less expensive, tutoring and other assistance is more readily available, and community colleges usually have a manageable payment plan in place for both full and part-time students. You can take one class at a time or go full time to complete your core courses, get an associate's degree, then transfer to the college or university of your choice to obtain a bachelor's degree and beyond.

- Scholarships aren't just for high school students. Look online for scholarships and grants for working moms, single moms, military wives, disenfranchised people, and more. Don't let worry over money stop you. Get creative. Where there is a will, there is always a way.

If you want more life in your life, volunteer.

- Local community centers, hospitals, and nonprofit organizations are always looking for people to donate a helping hand. Volunteers often get low-cost or free access to other programs the organization offers. Learn something new or teach something you already know. Make connections with some new people. Who knows, you may meet the love of your life—or at least have the time of your life—helping others.

- Join a gym or the local YWCA for exercise and camaraderie. Have kids and can't leave them at home? Download a free exercise app and workout with friends or family members at home. Get creative with the kids' playtime and join in the fun. Play a game of kickball or chase each other around the yard for a few minutes a day. You'll be amazed how being active and outside for as little as five minutes can lift your spirits.

Are you looking for your soul mate?

- Stop looking and concentrate on being the type of person you would like to go out with. Become more interesting by becoming more interested in the world around you. Laugh more. Smile more. Read. Dance. Sing. Whatever floats your boat. Challenge yourself to grow exponentially while you're waiting. Keep in mind that waiting doesn't mean standing still and doing nothing.

Multi-level marketing was one of the ways I learned a great deal about networking, marketing skills, and associations. Though it didn't work for me, feel free to try your hand at this type of business model. Make sure it is with a reputable company with a proven track record. Check the company's status with the Better Business Bureau and other reputable agencies. Don't just take someone's word for it. As with any business, do your due diligence.

Invest in yourself. Read through this book in its entirety then read it again. Underline, highlight, and take notes. Write down your ideas and organize your thoughts in a journal specifically for use while reading. Check out all the resources, references, and additional information, including the recommended videos, movies, and additional reading. The more you know, the faster you will grow.

Don't give up because of one bad chapter in your life. Each day is a new day. Each day is a blank page to the next chapter of your life.

You are the author – write your own story.

References

Amadeo, K. (2021, December 12). *Collateralized Debt Obligations (CDOs).* (M. J. Boyle, Ed.). The Balance. https://www.thebalance.com/cdos-collateralized-debt-obligations-3305822#:~:text=Key%20Takeaways%201%20Collateralized%20debate%20obligations%20%28CDOs%29%20are

Arax, M. (1993, May 4). COLUMN ONE : *The Child Brides of California* : *In the Central Valley, Hmong men continue the tradition of marrying girls as young as 12 or 13. Most of them quickly become welfare mothers. But some women are balking.* Los Angeles Times. https://www.latimes.com/archives/la-xpm-1993-05-04-mn-31160-story.html

Biali, S. (2015, November 4). *9 building blocks of a great life!* Complete Wellbeing. https://completewellbeing.com/article/9-building-blocks-of-a-great-life/

Blehart, M. "MJ. (2019, June 7). *Desire vs. Want.* Medium. https://mjblehart.medium.com/desire-vs-want-28c362978103

Bottaro, A. (2021, December 10). *What's The Difference Between a Stigma and a Stereotype?* Verywell Health. https://www.verywellhealth.com/stigma-vs-stereotype-5210852

Buhler, J. (2020). *Supporting Refugees in Thailand.* MCC Vietnam. https://www.rememberingmccvietnam.net/supporting-refugees-in-thailand

Cherry, K. (2019). *Milgram's Experiments and the Perils of Obedience.* Verywell Mind. https://www.verywellmind.com/the-milgram-obedience-experiment-2795243

Cherry, K. (2022, February 14). *The Five Levels of Maslow's Hierarchy of Needs.* Verywell Mind. Dotdash. https://www.verywellmind.com/what-is-maslows-hierarchy-of-needs-4136760

DeGrace, T. (2011, December 18). *The Housing Market Crash of 2007 and What Caused the Crash.* http://www.stockpickssystem.com/housing-market-crash-2007/

Desai, P. (2014, August 19). *The Power of Possibility.* HuffPost. https://www.huffpost.com/entry/the-power-of-possibility_b_5693332

Fleming, E. (2020, July 27). *How did the Hmong get to America?* SidmartinBio. https://www.sidmartinbio.org/how-did-the-hmong-get-to-america/

History.com Editors. (2018, August 21). *Han Dynasty.* HISTORY; A&E Television Networks. https://www.history.com/topics/ancient-china/han-dynasty

Hmong Association of Washington. (2010). *Our History*. Hmong Association of WA. https://www.hmongofwa.org/our-history.html

Langston Hughes. (1992). *The Panther & the Lash, Poems of our Times.* New York Vintage Books. (Original work published 1967)

Libreria Editrice Vaticana. (1984, May 11). *To refugees in the Camp of Phanat Nikhom*. John Paul II. https://www.vatican.va/content/john-paul-ii/en/speeches/1984/may/documents/hf_jp-ii_spe_19840511_campo-rifugiati.html

Lifey. (2020, April 3). *The truth about Hmong culture, history, food + language!* // Hmong vlog documentary. Video. https://www.youtube.com/watch?v=tK3GmQUnDwY&t=1s

Noah, T. (2019, October 3). *"Good Credit, Buy Anything!"* Trevor Noah. Video. https://www.youtube.com/watch?v=NvLtjOiMDYE&t=285s

Onelove. (2017, December 21). *11 Reasons Why People in Abusive Relationships Can't "Just Leave."* One Love Foundation. https://www.joinonelove.org/learn/why_leaving_abuse_is_hard/

Project Manager. (2013, July 29). *How to Work Smarter Not Harder.* Video. https://www.youtube.com/watch?v=VQx6L-EVJYM&t=497s

Raypole, C. (2020, June 11). *9 Ways To Kick Off Your Self-Discovery Journey*. Healthline. https://www.healthline.com/health/self-discovery#visualize

Sasson, R. (2022). *The Power of Imagination.* SuccessConsciousness. https://www.successconsciousness.com/blog/concentration-mind-power/power-of-imagination/

Seltzer, L. F. (2021, July 7). *How Do You Define Success?* Psychology Today. https://www.psychologytoday.com/us/blog/evolution-the-self/202107/how-do-you-define-success

Thorp, T. (2019, February 7). *How to Identify Your Soulmate.* Chopra. https://chopra.com/articles/how-to-identify-your-soulmate

Valentine, M. (2018, February 28). *3 Things Nobody Tells You About Love and Success.* Goalcast. https://www.goalcast.com/things-nobody-tells-you-about-love-and-success/

Wall Street Journal. (2020b, May 1). *What Happens to Landlords When Tenants Can't Pay Rent?* Wall Street Journal. Video. https://www.youtube.com/watch?v=V0Vwerb2JvE&t=3s

Wozniacka, G. (2012, June 11). *Hmong Women Break with Traditional Roles.* MPR News. https://www.mprnews.org/story/2012/06/11/hmong-women-break-with-traditional-roles

Yang, K. K. (2008). LitCharts. https://www.litcharts.com/lit/the-latehomecomer/chapter-6-phanat-nikhom-transition-camp-to-america